Zach + Dan
God bless
Dad

PRAISES FOR
MISSIONARY PARENTING

"Over the years Bob and Nannet Horton have helped many, many people come to know and love Christ and his Church and grow in their life of faith. They are true missionary disciples. Above all they have striven to live their married vocation as faithful and fruitful missionary parents for their children. They have written this book to help other married couples do the same. In *Missionary Parenting*, Bob and Nannet have assembled a treasury of wisdom from Scripture, Church teaching, liturgical prayer and the lived experience of everyday disciples to cast a vision for married couples to intentionally form their families as the domestic church. Each chapter focuses on one of six Christ-centered relationships that are essential for the family to fulfill its vocation. Readers will find in these pages a rich and encouraging road map to respond with greater generosity and confidence to God's plan of love for their family's life."

—Father Scott Traynor
Vicar for Lay and Clergy Formation
Diocese of Sioux Falls

"Bob and Nannet Horton have followed the Lord as a couple for a long time. I am delighted to see that they are making the wisdom gained from many years of marriage and family life available to all of us. An inspiring couple and an inspiring book."

—Ralph Martin, S.T.D.
President, Renewal Ministries
Director of Graduate Theology Programs in the New Evangelization
Sacred Heart Major Seminary
Archdiocese of Detroit

"The main challenge for Catholic parents in the 21st Century toxic culture is raising children to persevere in the Faith throughout the teen years and young adulthood. *Missionary Parenting* presents the six key relationships vital for passing on an enduring faith-life. St. John Paul II said, "The future of the world and of the Church passes through the family." This valuable book shows parents how passing on the Faith is done.

—Steve Wood
President, Family Life Center International

"As a father of 6, I have longed to see more parenting resources in the Catholic Church solidly and practically grounded in discipleship. Bob and Nannet are passionate and inspiring about fostering a deep love for Jesus in family life. They hang everything they outline on helpful illustrations and stories. Catholic parents will be on surer footing in raising solid disciples of Jesus if they read this book."

—Jason Simon
President, Evangelical Catholic

"A must-read primer for every Catholic family. Once you read it, put it back on top of the list and read it again!"

—Jon Leonetti
Catholic speaker and best-selling author

"Bob and Nannet have provided an inspiring vision of Catholic parenting. As a spouse, a parent, and one who works in marriage and family life ministry, I found this book to be a tremendous guide and resource for fostering missionary discipleship within the family."

—Matt Selby
Director of Marriage and Family Life
Archdiocese of Dubuque

MISSIONARY PARENTING

Cultivating the *6* Key Relationships Essential to Your Domestic Church

BOB AND NANNET HORTON

Nihil Obstat: Rev. Richard L. Schaefer
                   Censor Deputatus
                   June 4, 2020

Imprimatur: + Most Rev. Michael O. Jackels
                   Archbishop of Dubuque
                   June 18, 2020

The *nihil obstat* and *imprimatur* are official declarations
that a book or pamphlet is free of doctrinal or moral error.
No implication is contained herein that those who granted
the *nihil obstat* and *imprimatur* agree with the contents,
opinions, or statements expressed.

Copyright ©2020 Bob and Nannet Horton. All rights reserved.

No part of this publication may be reproduced, stored in a retrieval system,
or transmitted in any form or by any means, electronic, mechanical,
photocopying, recording, or otherwise, without the prior permission in
writing of the author.

Scripture passages are from the *New American Bible* © 1970, 1986, 1991, 2010
by the Confraternity of Christian Doctrine. All rights reserved.

References using "CCC" refer to the *Catechism of the Catholic Church*,
with the appropriate paragraph number. © 1994, 1997 by the United States
Catholic Conference, Inc.–Libreria Editrice Vaticana. Used by permission.
All rights reserved.

Cover art by Millet, Jean-François. *Potato Planters.* circa 1861.

Cover design and interior layout by Mike Fontecchio, Faith & Family
Publications.

For more information and to order, visit MissionaryParenting.com

ISBN: 978-1-7351265-0-0

Printed in the United States of America

DEDICATION

For Darci, Katherine, Theresa, Anna, Mark, Jubilee, and Mary who taught us truth, goodness, and beauty that only children can reveal.

CONTENTS

INTRODUCTION

"How precious is the family, as the privileged place for transmitting the faith."

—Pope Francis

Catch the Vision.

Father Evans did not anticipate being nearly tackled at Mass that Sunday morning as he began the entrance procession. A two-year-old boy named Augustine flung himself at the knees of the beloved priest to hug him, as the boy's father failed an attempted intervention. Father Evans regained his balance and smiled with delight at the enthusiastic greeting of the young parishioner. "C'mon, Augustine!" his father said, as he pried the boy's chubby fingers from the priest's green chasuble. He scooped up his son and whispered to the priest, "Sorry, Father." Everyone in church grinned with amusement, with one parishioner commenting, "I hope that boy will still be running into church fifteen years from now." Though said in jest, this is a sobering question. Will Augustine still embrace his Catholic faith as a teenager? As a young adult? Will he continue attending Mass or will he be running in the opposite direction? The statistics look grim.

Where Have All the Children Gone?

A recent study entitled *Going, Going, Gone: The Dynamics of Catholic Disaffiliation in Young Catholics*, indicates that thirteen is the median age when those who leave the Church stop identifying as Catholic.[1] Many of these youngsters stop identifying as Catholic even though they might still attend Mass with their families. Researchers sought to understand the reasons why young people leave the Church, and they discovered that the "disaffiliation" process happens over time, following a series of unresolved issues and experiences. Though the Church's teachings on sexuality and the clerical sexual abuse scandal are among the reasons given, these issues are not among the top three. Based on a wide sample of former Catholics in the United States aged fifteen to twenty-four, the most commonly reported reasons are:

1. No longer believe in God or religion

---

[1] St. Mary's Press / Center for Applied Research in the Apostolate, 2018

2. Parental or family influences

3. Changed to another religion

Actually, these reasons are nothing new. They are the same issues that led Catholics of generations past to stop practicing the Faith (the so-called "fallen away Catholics").

The first is easy to understand. Those who no longer believe in God or the value of organized religion would naturally consider the teachings and practices of the Church meaningless and therefore disaffiliate themselves.

The second includes a range of challenging life experiences such as divorce, illness, the imposition of the faith, and death. Numerous former Catholics disengage from the Church because of deep wounds from difficult relationships and painful family experiences.

The third indicates that many former Catholics join another religion for a variety of reasons. Perhaps an inadequate understanding of the fullness of the Catholic Faith fails to anchor them to the Church that Jesus established.

While findings in this recent study show a common thread with those who have left the Church in past generations, what is new in this study is the median age when those raised Catholic disaffiliated themselves from the Church—*thirteen*. This indeed is a shocking finding.

Thirteen year olds are still children in many ways and are already treading in spiritual poverty if they disaffiliated because of loss of faith or negative family impact. Each is a son or daughter of God who has been rendered spiritually imperiled at a tender age. If someone were to abduct our thirteen-year-old child, we would be devastated. How much more should we dread the spiritual damage to their soul.

Our minds struggle to understand how this could happen to our children and what we can do to prevent it. Many factors in our post-Christian culture besiege families and can snuff the flame of faith received at Baptism. The pervasiveness of relativism, the isolation of families, the breakdown in marriage, the emphasis on individualism, the pursuit of self-interests, faith alone in science and technology, and negative light on Christianity are just a few factors that impact people in our day. Ultimately, these factors are rooted in secularism, which promotes a life without God.

A major difference from past generations is that our children are exposed to falsehoods and deceptions at an increasingly younger age. We as Catholic parents need to actively lay a foundation of faith, hope, and love in our children's hearts and minds that will keep the flame burning brightly. This requires us to act as missionary parents.

Missionary Parenting

The primary solution to the exodus of our young people from the Faith lies within our grasp as parents. The Church calls upon parents to be the first educators and teachers of the faith to our children and to build a domestic church. Today, more than ever, we as parents must engage with our children in proactive and mindful ways, not acting out of fear but of hope in Christ and his grace. Parents must have clear sight of a missionary path to reach the hearts of our children for God and the Church.

God ordained the parent-child relationship to be the most influential early relationship in the lives of children. One longitudinal study shows, "No other conceivable causal influence ... comes remotely close to matching the influence of parents on the religious faith and practices of youth."[2] This is the good news that we as parents should understand and capitalize on. No matter what we and our children face in today's culture, our love for our children and the natural respect that they have for us can form the basis for a golden opportunity. Most importantly, God is on our side. We have the "home court advantage." The loving and faith-filled formation that we as Catholic parents can provide through the sensitive formative years of each child can have a lasting impact. Forming and nurturing a domestic church is bringing the kingdom of God into our homes, and planting a mustard seed in our children's hearts and minds that will take root and bear fruit.

You are reading this book because your Catholic faith is important to you. Clearly, you want to form your children in the Faith because you have experienced firsthand the truth, goodness, and beauty of a relationship with God that makes all the difference in your life. You committed to following Jesus and his Church, and you desire your children to experience the freedom and abundance of life in Christ. As a disciple, you aspire to effectively bring your relationship with Jesus into your domestic church.

---

[2] Smith and Snell, 2009

The Domestic Church

Christian parents sincerely desire to raise their children in the Faith. Desire alone, however, is not enough. Parents must have a *vision* for their family, with a clear picture of what it can become or ought to be. The domestic church, which is the family as the first faith community, is such a vision. At its core are *relationships* into which married couples deliberately integrate faith, hope, and love. This book presents six key relationships centered on Jesus Christ that, when developed and cultivated, actualize a domestic church.

The six essential relationships are:

1. between each parent and Jesus (personal discipleship)

2. between spouses (marital spirituality)

3. between parents and each child (missionary parenting)

4. between each family member (family spirituality)

5. between Jesus and each child (discipleship)

6. between the family and the universal Church (integration)

By highlighting the significance of these six relationships, this book presents a vision for the domestic church that will help you formulate a specific plan for your family. You will learn how to include your family in your personal discipleship with Jesus. You and your spouse will learn how to bring intentionality into your marital relationship, your relationship with your children, the relationship between every member of your family, and the relationship of your family with the universal Church. Discovering the Church's teachings on human nature, marriage, and the role of parents will enable you to design a family action plan—a plan that will strengthen the bonds between you and your children and your children with one another. It will help your family to become more aware of the presence of God in their lives and experience an outpouring of his grace. It is our hope that you will experience genuine hope on how to build your family as a faith community, a domestic church. It is love in relationships that has the power to raise the next generation of Catholics.

The Home Court Advantage

We, the authors are Catholic disciples who have a clear desire to be the first educators and teachers of the faith to our children. Because our Catholic faith is central to us, we want to raise our children to love and follow Jesus. We set our efforts on the vital elements of the Christian family vocation— deepening our marriage bond and helping our children open themselves to a relationship with God and his Church. We have struggled to find materials to help us build a loving and faith-filled family. We have written this book to help Catholic parents understand the importance of your role and influence on the spiritual lives of your children, the principal place of Jesus in family relationships, and the value of raising your children with the grace to respond in faith and love to Jesus and the Church.

Although there are many practical tips in this book, please do not read it as a self-help book, seeing the relational elements as merely actions you can incorporate into your plan. This book offers a blueprint for missionary parenting that establishes a domestic church. It is primarily a *vision* book. The vision for families is a network of strong and loving relationships with God, each other and the Church. Remember that a relationship with Jesus is central to each of the six essential relationships. All actions in your plan must flow from your loving relationship with Jesus in cooperation with the Holy Spirit. Parents can catch the vision and tailor the elements of relationships discussed in this book to the needs of your particular family. Along with a vision, examples of real families (the names have been changed) are provided to equip Catholic couples with the focus, confidence, courage, and joy to become missionary parents.

As a disciple of Jesus, you already hold the first key, which is your relationship with him.

Chapter One

BE A CATHOLIC DISCIPLE

*"The Christian faith is, above all, conversion to
Jesus Christ, full and sincere adherence to his person
and the decision to walk in his footsteps."*

—General Directory for Catechesis, 53

Be the Seed that Dies.

As a university freshman, Rebecca delved deeply into her university's Greek culture and its partying as she enjoyed her first year of living away from home. Just before her parents arrived to visit her at college for the first time, she checked out the local Catholic parish. Rebecca noted the Sunday Mass times so she would know when she and her parents could attend during their visit. In the church, she noticed a flyer for a parish event that interested her, and she decided to attend the event alone because she did not know anyone at the parish. It was a program where a speaker shared his faith testimony. His personal story deeply touched Rebecca, as the man spoke about turning his life over to the Lord following the accidental death of his one-year-old daughter. This reminded Rebecca of a younger sibling who died many years ago, and how an older sister shielded her from their mother's extended period of grief and depression. This realization led her to face the effects of her family's struggles on her own life. For the first time, Rebecca turned to God to seek healing and transformation. The campus ministry in the local parish helped her to become a true disciple of Jesus Christ.

Each disciple of Jesus has a unique story of a life-changing encounter with him. Jesus reveals himself in a profoundly personal and meaningful way, and one responds to his call. This response includes turning away from sinful habits and turning towards Jesus to follow him in a new life in the Spirit. Saying *yes* to Jesus is being that seed that falls on the ground and dies so that a new life can begin (see John 12:24).

To become a disciple of Jesus entails a *decision*, similar to what is needed to enter into a relationship with a person. Many Catholics or those who have been baptized as infants may not yet have made a personal adult decision to be in a relationship with Jesus. If you have already made a decision to follow Jesus and commit your life to him, you are living a life of discipleship. If you have not yet made that choice, seriously consider right now to enter into a relationship with Jesus who loves you and gave his life on the Cross for the forgiveness of your sins and freedom to live an abundant life. Jesus is alive today. Talk to him and express your desire to be in a holy relationship with him. Ask for the grace to repent of sin, and ask Jesus to come into your heart as Lord and Savior. Jesus wants to be in a loving relationship with you, "Behold, I stand at the door and knock. If anyone hears my voice and opens the door, I will enter his house and dine with him, and he with me" (Revelation 3:20).

By choosing to follow Jesus, you begin a relationship with him that opens up a life of faith. With the eyes of faith, you start to perceive the natural and supernatural as one complete reality, and your new-found relationship with Jesus fosters a unity of your body and spirit. You begin to grow in your interior knowledge of God's love for you, and you have an increasing desire to seek him. Making time in your daily life for God becomes a priority. The regular communication with Jesus opens you up to spiritual growth, and this will gradually and progressively bear much fruit. A life of faith is a fruitful life. The lives of the apostles, saints, and holy men and women in the Church over the past two millennia beautifully demonstrate the abundance of life in Jesus. Like the saints, a true disciple of Jesus has a personal faith in him and strives for intentional discipleship within the Church.

Discipleship and the Domestic Church

A relationship with Jesus is the first key relationship essential to the domestic church, because the fullest loving relationships in the family are possible only in him, through him, and with him.

A relationship with Jesus is essential because it becomes the foundation of all familial relationships. Relationships make up the fabric of life and make it worth living; however, sin breaks relationships.

The gravest and most damaging effect of original sin was spiritual death, and separation from God. What original sin did was break the most foundational relationship, the relationship between humans and God. It is like a crack on a car windshield caused by the impact of a pebble. A seemingly small break will continue to spread in different directions on the windshield unless it is repaired immediately. Because the relationship with God was the basis of all other relationships, those other relationships splintered and fell to pieces. The relationship between man and woman, parents and children, siblings with each other were all torn apart as illustrated by the account in Genesis. The relationship with God is the first relationship that needs to be reconciled.

As Jesus says, "I am the way and the truth and the life. No one comes to the Father except through me" (John 14:6). The death of Jesus on the Cross was required to reconcile sinners to God. When the relationship with God is restored, all other relationships can come to proper order as well. What sin separates, the love of Jesus reconnects, and the power of the Holy Spirit binds. Holy family relationships begin, grow and bear fruit in a domestic church.

The domestic church is a community of relationships in which the relationship with Jesus Christ is primary. Even as a married disciple of Jesus with a family, Jesus remains the central person in your life. Your relationships with your spouse, children, and extended family all hinge upon your relationship with Jesus. Without first being a disciple, you cannot be a missionary parent. Jesus, you (as disciple), and the Church are essential elements of a domestic church. Building your domestic church on the foundation of Jesus and his Church is simply an expansion of your discipleship in Christ.

Discipleship is a relationship that entails listening to Jesus, attending to his presence, and seeking his will. Before committing your life to Christ, you focused on your needs, desires, and opinions, but after committing to Christ, your life gained a new center. A remarkable change that happens in the disciple's heart is the significant shift to an interior disposition to *receive* from Jesus, to be *formed* in love. As your relationship with Jesus deepens, your capacity to listen, seek, and obey increases your ability to love God and others. Following Jesus is a great privilege, "Turning to the disciples in private, Jesus said, "Blessed are the eyes that see what you see. For I say to you, many prophets and kings desired to see what you see, but did not see it, and to hear what you hear, but did not hear it" (Luke 10:23-24). You become not only a hearer of the Word but also a doer of the Word. To love Jesus helps you become less self-centered, which, in turn, improves your ability to love your spouse and children more fully.

The interior disposition to receive from Jesus also disposes you to receive from his Church. This new receptivity allows you to fully draw all of the intended graces from the sacraments to live a fruitful life. This proper disposition enables you to receive the graces that God provides through the ordinary and extraordinary means. Much grace is required to love your spouse and children and to build your domestic church. A receptivity to grace grows as you mature in a life of discipleship.

Life of Discipleship

When Jesus walked the earth, he formed his disciples in the three years that he was with them. Jesus lived with them, mentored them in his public ministry, and instructed them privately as they followed him. His approach was the human approach that engaged the disciples in mind, body, and spirit. Jesus' approach was relational, communal, formative, and spiritual. It is no accident that after Jesus ascended into heaven and the Holy Spirit descended on Pentecost, the thousands of newly baptized Christians formed a community that lived a similar life of discipleship. "They devoted themselves to the teaching of the apostles and to the communal life, to the breaking of the bread and to the prayers. ... They would sell their property and possessions and divide them among all according to each one's need" (Acts 2:42, 45). The new followers of Jesus engaged in prayer, liturgy, catechesis, communal life and charity work. Discipleship today takes on the same elements because it is Jesus and the Holy Spirit who form the disciple.

Catholic Discipleship Schema

The following Catholic Discipleship Schema is a diagram that shows the essential components of the life of a disciple. These components are the new desires that flow like rays from a relationship with Jesus and the fruit of graces received in the sacraments. These effects of grace lead the disciple along a trajectory of loving God and loving others. At the same time, these are actions the disciple incorporates in her life to grow intentionally in that trajectory. Jesus' life had these components as he lived entirely in loving God and others.

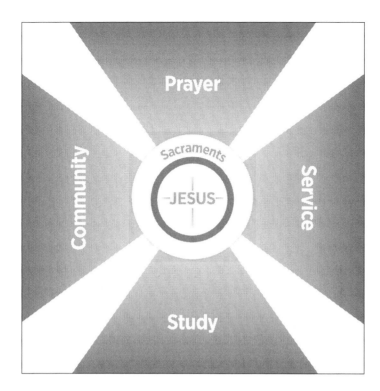

Catholic Discipleship Schema

- The relationship with Jesus holds the center of a disciple's life.
- The sacraments of the Church are central to the life of the disciple.
- Prayer is where the relationship gets personal.
- The study of Scripture and the Faith increases the disciple's knowledge and understanding.
- Community provides the disciple a clear path to be part of a large group and participate in communal life.
- Service to others enables a disciple to be a servant like Jesus in the world.

These components in a disciple's life facilitate deeper conversion to Jesus and spiritual transformation.

Relationship with Jesus

Everyone can have a relationship with God because he creates each person out of love and for love. In Baptism, this relationship takes a filial character as God adopts you as his son or daughter. With this adoption, you share with Jesus the Father's love and favor for his Son.

Choosing to be a disciple activates your end of this filial connection. The relationship with Jesus becomes vital because it is in union with him that Jesus "shares" his being-a-son-of-God-the-Father with you. The crucial thing about discipleship is that you allow Jesus to form you after his own heart. He conforms in you the love and obedience and goodwill that he has for God the Father.

This love relationship will demand your whole heart, mind, soul, and strength. It will conform you to the cross of Christ. It is on the Cross where the mystery of death and new life happens, where the seed dies, and a new life begins. God the Father on his part meets the demand of this love and wholly gives you his Son, the Holy Spirit, and his own divine life and love. From this mutual, free, and total self-donation, you enter into a genuine love relationship with God himself.

- A few weeks, following the parish event where the speaker's testimony touched her heart, Rebecca felt a renewed interest in the Catholic Faith of her childhood, and she began attending Mass. One Sunday, she noticed an advertisement for a weekend retreat for college students, and she decided to sign up. At the retreat, Rebecca experienced a community of young people with hearts open to God. She had the opportunity to respond more fully to Jesus' call to her, and she committed her life to Christ that weekend. In the remaining years of her college life, the Holy Spirit led her to a transformation through discipleship.

The Sacraments and Discipleship

The sacraments are visible signs of an interior grace instituted by Christ to grant grace. Grace is God's own divine life. The sacraments are also central to the life of the disciple because they are actual encounters with Jesus. From the sacraments, the disciple draws grace for the spiritual journey and parenting with a mission. By preparing the mind and heart each time before receiving a sacrament, a disciple comes to the proper interior disposition. The disciple is thus more open to receiving the intended grace of the sacrament, which will bear fruit in her life.

For the disciple of Jesus, the Church is the Body of Christ. As the Catechism states, "Christ and his Church together make up the *whole Christ*—Christus totus" (CCC 795). A relationship with Jesus, therefore, means a relationship with the Church. Following Jesus means following the Church. A growing love and fidelity to the Catholic Church usually happen for the disciple, and it becomes common for a disciple to desire to receive the sacraments often. The sacraments of the Church are encounters with Jesus in a concrete way, not only in words but also in material elements. As Jesus manifested the divine to us by becoming a man, the Church makes God present to us with blessed "matter" of the sacraments. In the Church, a disciple comes to union with Jesus and his Body.

- Rebecca discovered that many of her fellow students would visit the student lounge at the parish provided for college students. She began to go there in between her classes and met many students who were also trying to live their Catholic Faith. The friendships Rebecca formed with other students and their witness of faith encouraged her tremendously. Not only did she begin to attend Sunday Mass every week, she also began attending Mass on weekdays whenever her class schedule allowed it. She found that she experienced a growing desire to receive Jesus in the Eucharist.

There is one sacrament, Confirmation, that particularly comes to life when a Catholic chooses to become a disciple. Confirmation initiates a person more fully into the life of the Church through an outpouring of the Holy Spirit. For many adult Catholics, this sacrament seems somewhat obscure and almost forgotten. Baptism is easily remembered as the sacrament that removes original sin and initiates a person into God's family. The awareness of sin reminds Catholics to celebrate the sacrament of Reconciliation. The Holy Eucharist highlights communion with Jesus through reception of his body and blood at Mass. Confirmation, however, is received only once, usually as a teenager (in the Roman rite, at least), and this sacrament is seldom mentioned again. Discipleship renews a relationship with the Holy Spirit and stirs the graces from this much overlooked but powerful sacrament of initiation.

In Confirmation, we are "sealed with the gift of the Holy Spirit" which strengthens us for service to the Body of Christ. The Holy Spirit gives us the increased ability to practice our Catholic faith and to witness Christ in every situation. For most Catholics, the grace from this sacrament remains dormant because of a lack of engagement with the Holy Spirit. However, the Spirit continues to draw us to Christ and salvation. When we, as disciples, embark on the spiritual journey of following Jesus, we "wake up" to the presence of the Holy Spirit and follow his promptings and leading. The Spirit provides the power that actively forms our minds and hearts.

Jesus is the one who "baptizes you with the Holy Spirit and fire" (Matthew 3:11). In Confirmation, we renew our baptismal promises and accept the articles of the Catholic Faith expressed in the Creed. During the rite, the bishop, who is consecrated to act *in persona Christi Capitis* ("in the person of Christ the Head")—that is, with the authority of Jesus himself—extends his hand over our heads. In effect, it is Jesus who extends his hand over us. This gesture is a visible sign of a spiritual reality; that is, Jesus imparting the Holy Spirit to us. This means that he immerses us in his Spirit and floods our heart with love, "The love of God has been poured out into our hearts through the Holy Spirit that has been given to us" (Romans 5:5). With extended hands, the bishop prays,

All-powerful God,

Father of our Lord Jesus Christ, by water and the Holy Spirit

you freed your sons and daughters from sin and gave them new life.

Send your Holy Spirit upon them to be their helper and guide.

We also receive unique spiritual gifts when the bishop continues to pray:

Give them the spirit of wisdom and understanding,

the spirit of right judgment and courage, the
spirit of knowledge, and reverence.

Fill them with the spirit of wonder and awe in your presence.

We ask this through Christ, our Lord. Amen.

The bishop anoints us on the forehead with holy chrism as he says, "*Be sealed with the Holy Spirit.*" And we respond, "*Amen.*"

In Baptism, we receive the theological virtues of faith, hope, and love to begin our life as a child in the family of God. In Confirmation, we receive the gifts of the Holy Spirit: wisdom, understanding, counsel, fortitude, knowledge, piety, and fear of the Lord. God gives these gifts to help us grow in personal holiness, for unity with the body of Christ, and to be a witness of Christ's love to others in the world, particularly in the mission to which we are called. The Holy Spirit at work in our minds, hearts, and spirits bears fruit. The fruit of the Holy Spirit: love, joy, peace, patience, kindness, generosity, faithfulness, gentleness, self-control (see Galatians 5:22-23), grows interiorly and manifests in our choices, behavior, and relationships. Moreover, Jesus sends the Holy Spirit to be our teacher, helper, and comforter. With the Holy Spirit, he "clothes you with power from on high" (Luke 24:49).

In essence, the sacrament of Confirmation is meant to serve as a "personal Pentecost" for each of us. The coming of the Holy Spirit upon us is as real as the tongues of fire that came upon the apostles and Mary on the first Pentecost. Becoming a disciple of Jesus is a renewal of our affiliation with the Holy Spirit. We begin to be open to the gifts, the work, and the presence of the Holy Spirit in us, with us, and through us. It works like the transmission in a car, which "transmits" the power from the engine to the wheels, so that they can move. Discipleship activates our ability to be open to the Holy Spirit, who provides us the power to love and live a holy life. These are the effects of a life open to Jesus and the Holy Spirit that are essential for the domestic church.

Prayer

Prayer is opening your hearts and minds to God and coming into his presence. It is in prayer that your interpersonal relationship and communication with Jesus happens. You are always in the presence of God because he is omnipresent, but that fact itself is not prayer because there is no engagement on your part. It is similar to a father in a room watching his child, but the child remains oblivious to his presence. You can be in the presence of God but not be attentive to him. It is like sharing a meal with a loved one, but rather than having a real conversation, you are scrolling down on your smartphone while the loved one talks to you. Personal prayer is directly engaging in the moment of the relationship, and an exchange takes place.

Any relationship needs essential communication, both verbal and nonverbal. A disciple cannot be formed without prayer. Prayer is relational between you and God, and it requires your active participation. It involves "the raising of one's mind and heart to God" (CCC 2590). It need not always have to include words. St. Therese of Lisieux describes prayer as "... a surge of the heart; it is a simple look turned toward heaven; it is a cry of recognition and love" (see CCC 2558). For the disciple with the interior disposition, prayer entails a waiting on and listening to God, no matter what method of prayer you choose.

For the Catholic, there is a variety of ways to communicate with God. The methods include vocal, mental, and contemplative prayer, the use of devotionals such as the Rosary and novenas, the Liturgy of the Hours, and *lectio divina,* which uses the Scriptures to pray. One may pray in song and groans, or even through the charism of speaking in tongues. There are personal prayers and communal prayer, of which the Mass is "source and summit" (CCC 1324). Prayer not only fosters and maintains a personal relationship with Jesus, but it makes intimacy with him possible.

- As the demands of academics and her sorority activities filled her schedule, Rebecca began to struggle in her prayer life. At first, she committed to recite a morning offering before her day began and to talk to Jesus as she went about her day. As she received the Eucharist frequently, she found that prayer became easier and more joyful as she grew in her relationship with Christ. In her second year at college, Rebecca let go of some of her sorority activities so that she could commit to a weekly holy hour of Eucharistic adoration at her parish.

To grow as a disciple, you do not only recite prayers, but you nurture a prayer life. After all, a disciple is one whom Jesus forms, like clay in the hands of the potter. In the Christian life, this does not happen without a deepening experience of prayer, without intimacy with Jesus. Besides a personal relationship with him, Jesus provided his followers with the Scriptures and the Church so that discipleship could be possible even when he no longer walked the earth. Jesus provides each disciple with many ways and means to draw closer to him.

Study

For a disciple, study is born out of a desire to know Jesus more and to learn how to live the Christian life. Study is the engagement of the intellect in the search for truth. Faith brings light, and reason brings the basis for understanding.

Study is a lifelong venture for the disciple because the knowledge of God and the mysteries of the faith are inexhaustible.

How can you love someone you do not know? As St. Paul exhorts the Christians in Rome, "Do not conform yourselves to this age but be transformed by the renewal of your mind, that you may discern what the will of God is, what is good and pleasing and perfect" (Romans 12:2). The renewal of the mind brought about by study helps you to know God, seek his will, and receive guidance that the Church provides. Growing in knowledge and understanding of spiritual matters informs the will and directs you to choose rightly. For the disciple, the Holy Spirit is the teacher who leads you to the truth. Study takes the disciple to more in-depth knowledge and understanding of God that brings forth fruits of wisdom and right judgment. For the disciple, Sacred Scripture becomes a significant means of "listening" to God.

Together, Sacred Scripture and Sacred Tradition are the sources of God's revelation as taught authoritatively by the Church. Sacred Scripture is the handing down of the Gospel message in *writing* by the apostles and men associated with the apostles, under the inspiration of the Holy Spirit (CCC 76). "Ignorance of Scripture is ignorance of Christ," insists St. Jerome (347–420), a Doctor of the Church and one of her greatest Scripture scholars. Sacred Tradition is the handing down of the Gospel message "by the spoken word of the apostles' preaching, by the example they gave, by the institutions they established, what they themselves had received - whether from the lips of Christ, from his way of life and his works, or whether they had learned it at the prompting of the Holy Spirit" (CCC 76). Sacred Scripture and Sacred Tradition have one source, and together, they make up a single sacred deposit of the faith.

Through its *magisterium* (or "teaching authority"), the Church's dogmatic teachings on faith and morality are clear and true. A Catholic disciple, then, grows to trust the Church's teachings and strives to conform her life to them.

The *Catechism of the Catholic Church*, papal encyclicals and apostolic letters, and other official Church documents are readily available online as resources for study. Other sources of study include the shared wisdom, reflections, and insights into the spiritual life from many holy men and women of the Church. All of these materials foster knowledge about God, the Church, faith, and the Christian life. They inform the mind of the disciple toward a deeper understanding of reality.

- Due to her leadership skills, Rebecca held some leadership positions in her sorority. She began to see conflicts in morality between some of her activities and her Catholic faith. In many of the parties and celebrations she attended, alcohol consumption and casual sexual encounters were the norm, as the motto was, "You are in college only once!" By taking advantage of the many opportunities and instructions offered to college students by her parish, Rebecca attended sessions on the Theology of the Body and gained a deeper understanding of her sexuality and holy relationships. This helped her make better choices for herself with regards to relationships.

A disciple needs to discern the content of study materials to determine if they align with the teachings of the Church before integrating them into her Christian life. There is wisdom in talking to a priest or more mature disciples who can shed light on your questions and concerns about some study content. Besides having resource persons, a disciple can find support and accountability in a community of people who are following Jesus.

Community

Community means engagement with a group of other disciples. Jesus chose twelve apostles to form a small community that he discipled for three years. As Jesus says, "For where two or three are gathered together in my name, there am I in the midst of them" (Matthew 18:20). Disciples can experience special graces in community. The community provides Christian fellowship, which forms spiritual brotherhood and sisterhood. Being in a small group helps a disciple have a network with other disciples, all of whom are striving to live their Christian lives faithfully. Mature disciples in the community can mentor newer disciples. More importantly, a community allows disciples to grow in love. As Jesus forms a disciple after his own heart, he conforms the heart to his love for others. The unity and love in a community stand as a witness to the presence of Jesus in their midst.

Small groups may be found in parishes or organized by disciples themselves. Many meet regularly for study and prayer. Many groups also include a service component.

- For her third year of college, Rebecca decided to room with a few female college students with whom she had formed Christian friendships. She continued to be inspired by Catholic women in the small faith-sharing group that she joined at the parish. Many of the young women had experienced faith conversions, and even with the struggles they faced in college, relationships, and their families, their Christian friendships were sources of hope and encouragement.

The Catholic Faith involves both personal faith and communal faith, and a disciple needs other Christians to grow properly.

Service

Service refers to voluntary efforts provided for others. For a disciple, service is a work of love. The transformative power of following Jesus manifests in lovingly witnessing to others in words and actions. God gives different gifts to various persons, and in the community, the disciple has opportunities to offer her gifts for the common good. The disciple also serves those who are within her scope of life. With the eyes and ears of faith, a disciple begins to see and hear people in a new way. She becomes more sensitive to their needs and is moved by mercy to help them.

The disciple begins to understand Jesus' identification of himself with the sufferings of others, "Amen, I say to you, whatever you did for one of these least brothers of mine, you did for me" (Matthew 25:40).

- Rebecca had attended Catholic elementary and high schools, and everything she had learned about the Catholic Faith now became *real* to her; before, it was only information. Her love of Jesus awakened in her an appreciation and understanding of all she had learned about the Faith. Grateful to have her faith renewed, she volunteered to help in the parish RCIA program to welcome inquirers considering joining the Church.

The disciple serves to meet the practical needs and spiritual needs of others, following the corporal and spiritual works of mercy. A disciple is called to meet them in love and compassion as part of growing in her relationship with Christ.

The Catholic Discipleship Schema is a tool that shows the essential components of Catholic discipleship. These components are fruits of a relationship with Jesus and graces from the sacraments as well as actions the disciple takes to grow in discipleship. Spiritual maturity is a lifelong process of growing in love. To incorporate these components in your life is to grow in loving God and loving others. A relationship with Jesus, the graces from the sacraments, prayer, study, community, and service help you to engage fully in the Christian life. The engagement of mind, heart, body, and relationships brings an integration that conforms you more and more to Jesus Christ.

Vocation

There is a specific call that Jesus issues to each Catholic disciple—namely, a *vocation*. For Catholics, vocation is not just any call; it is a call from God. God calls a disciple to a commitment to love him in a particular way. The Church recognizes four vocations: priesthood, consecrated religious life, marriage, and blessed singlehood. Unlike careers, vocations are invitations from God who made each person, knows each person, and has in mind the highest good for each person. Each vocation leads a disciple on a path to holiness. Within each vocation, God calls the disciple to particular works for the kingdom of God. As St. Paul explains, "For we are his handiwork, created in Christ Jesus for the good works that God has prepared in advance, that we should live in them" (Ephesians 12:10). Part of discipleship is listening for the vocational call of God.

- By the time she graduated from college, Rebecca was practicing her Catholic Faith with a renewed zeal, a love for Jesus and a servant's heart. She had met a young man who was also committed to his faith, and they discerned a call to marriage. They are now married and aspire to build their family as a domestic church.

You discerned the marriage vocation and entered the sacrament of Matrimony with another disciple. Marriage is a call to an intimate community of love and life called the *family*. You and your spouse witness to the love and presence of God by generously receiving children and educating them. Your marriage vocation is an expansion of your discipleship. If the disciple is "being the seed," then vocation is the garden into which the seed is sown—to die, to grow, and to bear fruit.

Deny Yourself, Pick up Your Cross, and Follow Jesus

A disciple always contends with a tension between what you want to do and what Jesus is calling you to do. Many times, this tension becomes a real battle. St. Augustine says, "There can only be two basic loves ... the love of God to the forgetfulness of self, or the love of self to the forgetfulness and denial of God."

The denial of yourself is giving up your desires, plans, and control of your life so that you can be free to become like Jesus. This is never easy, as it may call you out of your comfort zone or require you to give up favorite attachments. Picking up your cross means making sacrifices out of love for God and others. To follow Jesus is to imitate his way of humility and complete trust in the Father. To put total confidence in God is to acknowledge that he knows you and has your best interest in mind no matter the circumstances you face. Although this tension or battle happens interiorly, the outcome manifests exteriorly in the choices you make. Grace in this internal tug-o-war comes in putting your faith in the goodness of God, trusting in the faithfulness of Jesus, and leaning on the power of the Holy Spirit for strength, perseverance, and courage to choose the way of love. As the Gospel of John puts it, "He [Jesus] must increase, and I must decrease" (John 3:30).

Sprouting Seeds

A life of discipleship is marked by a rhythm of death and new life. The seed that dies produces a new plant that does not look anything like the seed from which it came. Only God can give life. New life has a promise that gradually unfolds until it reaches maturity. Many factors, including those unforeseen, contribute to the growth and development of the plant until it reaches its full potential. The mature plant has its beauty and purpose, but every step of its growth has its own extraordinary wonder. In the path of discipleship, you will go through many small deaths so that new life may sprout. Often, these "deaths" you experience occur in meeting the demands of love in relationships. Of all human relationships, marriage challenges us the most with the demands of spousal love.

TIME TO TALK

1. Share your personal faith story with your spouse. Describe your encounter with Jesus and how you responded to him.

2. Do you have a daily prayer life? Schedule a daily prayer time.

3. What is the best part of your discipleship right now? What areas in your heart do you need to more fully surrender to Jesus?

PRAYER

*Jesus, today, I renew my commitment to follow you
with my whole mind, soul, heart, and strength.
Please forgive me of my sins. Help me to know more
deeply the Father's love for me as his child. Fill me
with your Holy Spirit. Holy Spirit, renew in me the
fire of your love. I ask this in Jesus' name, Amen.*

Chapter Two

NURTURE A CATHOLIC MARITAL SPIRITUALITY

*"The love of husband and wife is the force
that welds society together."*

—St. John Chrysostom

Grow deep roots.

Like many couples, we (the authors) differ from one another in temperament, personality, family of origin, and cultural background. When we met, though, both of us were committed Catholic disciples of Jesus and open to the Holy Spirit in our lives. Before our wedding, we wrote down a two-part vision for our marriage. It was a declaration that together we were choosing a Christian way of life based on loving God and loving others. It stated our intention to live out the Great Commandments, not only within our marriage and family but also with others. At the time, we did not fully realize that this was the beginning of our marital spirituality. We still re-read our original vision statement on our wedding anniversary. Through it all, we thank God for his faithfulness and grace in our marriage.

A domestic church truly begins when a baptized man and baptized woman enter the sacrament of Matrimony. God created us male and female, equal in dignity and value. In God's plan, sacramental marriage is an intimate communion of a man and a woman that is indissoluble until death. Catholic disciples merge individual journeys of discipleship and together, follow Jesus. The *I* becomes *we*, and *my* becomes *our*. God has a specific plan for your marriage. By allowing God to dwell in your married love, you give God the chance to mold your marriage into his original design – two persons becoming one. This path involves listening together to his voice, and it is in this turning to God together that a husband and wife form a true marital spirituality.

Marital Spirituality and the Domestic Church

While a relationship between Jesus and his disciple is the first key relationship essential to the domestic church, the second is marital spirituality. It refers to the relationship between spouses and their relationship with Jesus. A domestic church is the first faith community for the family. Marital spirituality manifests a unity between husband and wife that forms marriage into the first community of faith. It refers to the clear choice that married disciples of Jesus embark on to live the unitive and procreative purposes of marriage as God's design. The intimate communion of persons in marriage happens when there is a mutual and total self-gift between spouses. God intends marriage to include the good of spouses, the transmission of life, and the education of children—and, ultimately, cooperation with the work of God. These purposes are directed towards the salvation of spouses and their children. It becomes imperative for disciples to have a marital spirituality to fulfill the purposes of marriage. Without a marital spirituality, the marriage relationship does not include a mutually lived, comprehensive spiritual component. Unity in spirituality is an essential element for the spiritual leadership of the faith community.

Prerequisites for Marital Spirituality

Two things are necessary for married disciples to develop and nurture a Catholic marital spirituality:

1. An *understanding* of the Catholic vision for marriage. This might mean studying Catholic teachings and discerning how to integrate them into your marriage.

2. A *desire* to live out the Catholic vision for marriage in your marital relationship. Here, an explicit agreement between spouses to work together is ideal.

Both an understanding and a desire to live out the Church's vision give rise to practical actions in implementing a plan for your marital spirituality. As St. John Paul II writes in *Love and Responsibility*, "God allows man to learn his supernatural ends, but the decision to strive towards an end, the choice, of course, is left to man's free will. God does not redeem man against his will."[3] The desire for God in your marriage becomes a choice to involve him and his will in your spousal relationship. This desire and choice must manifest in your actions. St. John Paul II expresses this concept in this way: "Love is never something ready-made, something merely 'given' to man and woman, it is always at the same time a 'task' to which they are set. Love should be seen as something which in a sense, never 'is' but is always only 'becoming.' What it becomes depends upon the contribution of both persons and the depth

---

[3] Karol Wojtyla (St. John Paul II), *Love and Responsibility* (San Francisco: Ignatius Press, 1993), p. 27

of their commitment." Couples need the formation of minds and hearts on marriage to assume the Catholic vision for marriage.

The Catholic Vision for Marriage

The communion-of-persons characteristic of a Catholic marriage rests on two essential properties—*unity* and *indissolubility*. Unity means that the sacramental bond is exclusive in a monogamous relationship. Indissolubility of the sacramental marriage involves two people who are faithful to one another until death, and the union is not dissolvable by any human authority. The Church regards marriage simultaneously as a vocation, a covenant, and a sacrament.

Marriage as a Vocation

The vocation to marriage is a call to total self-donation between spouses. God created man and woman for union with each other, so they are naturally drawn to one another. The marriage vocation has a unique attribute that Catholic disciples must understand clearly and accept as part of the vocation: sexual union. Sexuality plays a significant role in marriage because it is only in marriage that the sexual union is part of the vocation. The gift of the body to a spouse is a significant part of the total self-gift in marriage. Those called to blessed singlehood, consecrated religious life, and the priesthood, on the other hand, profess vows of celibacy.

- As a disciple of Christ, Alex was discerning his vocation. He decided to join a priesthood discernment group for college students at his local parish. There, young men, guided by the pastor, discuss and pray about the priestly vocation. After a year, Alex discerned that God was not calling him to the priesthood. Soon, he met a young woman, and they began dating. After they had been dating for a few months, they decided to discern marriage. Because Alex had learned the benefit of discerning God's call from the priest discernment group, he and his girlfriend asked the authors if we could meet with them regularly to discuss and pray with them about a vocation to marriage. We were impressed by their desire to discern God's call. (In the end, they did discern God was calling them to marriage.)

Understanding marriage as your vocation is essential for developing a marital spirituality. You are called to give yourself fully and exclusively in spousal love to a particular person. Learning and understanding your spouse, not only as a man or woman but also as the unique person that he or she is, becomes a daily task. This ongoing venture also allows you to help each other grow in holiness and love. Ultimately, a Catholic disciple's vocation of being a helpmate is to help your spouse grow in holiness on earth and upon death, to spend eternity in heaven.

Marriage as a Covenant

Couples enter into a covenant with each other and with God when they marry. A Christian marriage is a covenantal relationship because couples enter into it unconditionally. Together, a husband and a wife profess a lifelong commitment of unconditional love to each other that ends only by death. This covenant begins during the wedding ceremony, with the exchange of vows, but couples live it out in the daily choices throughout their lives—"for better, for worse, for richer, for poorer, in sickness and in health, to love and to cherish till death us do part."

It is helpful to consider St. John Paul II's insights on love as expressed in *Love and Responsibility*. He explains that love has both subjective and objective aspects. The subjective element includes the thoughts, feelings, and sensations experienced by a man or woman in a relationship. John Paul regards this as merely "a psychological situation," an experience happening *inside* a person. The objective aspect of the relationship refers to the reality of the relationship between the two involved persons. The Holy Father writes that the powerful sensations in a relationship can mask its reality. In some ways, this may even hinder the full development of the relationship. The subjective aspect is important, but in marriage, a covenantal relationship must go beyond the merely subjective to develop the objective element.

The objective aspect of a marriage is the development of the relationship towards a serious commitment to each other. This commitment includes an understanding of what is truly best for the other and having the faith and virtue for unity towards a common aim. St. John Paul II mentions that true love is an "impersonal fact," which seeks the highest good of another for their sake.[4]

The Holy Father insightfully writes that the sexual relationship presents more opportunities than most other activities for treating a person, even

---

[4] *Love and Responsibility*, pp. 82-100

unintentionally, as an object. Christian husbands and wives must nurture and develop the objective aspect of marriage with the help of the Holy Spirit to avoid this danger and grow in genuine love for their spouse.

Marriage as a covenant is a crucial understanding for marital spirituality because it calls you to fidelity to each other throughout your lives. As the *Catechism* puts it, "The covenant between the spouses is integrated into God's covenant with man. Authentic married love is caught up into divine love" (CCC 1639).

- Joe and Felicia raised their children and later in their marriage, Felicia developed a mental illness that incapacitated her. Joe had the choice to care for her at home or place her in a nursing home. He decided to care for her at home, and he served her many needs as a result of her illness. Joe chose to live out his wedding vows, despite a culture that encourages easy divorce and places a premium on self-fulfillment.

Marriage as a Sacrament

Jesus elevated marriage to be a sacrament. Why? Because, in calling two disciples to become one, marriage is an image of the Holy Trinity. The Trinity—the mystery of God being one in a communion of three Persons—is the central mystery of the Catholic Faith. A husband and wife increasingly become united as they share their lives and participate in a complete exchange of life and love. Marriage not only reflects the mystery of the Blessed Trinity but disciples also participate in the divine life of the Holy Trinity.

In a Christian marriage, the love of husband and wife for each other goes beyond human love. Whereas human love has a beauty achieved by human effort, Christian love grows by grace to go beyond the limits of human endeavor. One cannot love like Jesus without a heart like his heart. As with the other sacraments, the grace of the sacrament of Matrimony provides couples the ability to love like Jesus loves his Church.

The love of husband and wife reaches beyond merely human love to become conformed to the pattern of Jesus' love for his Bride, the Church, a love that is free, total, faithful and fruitful. These four attributes of the love of Christ comprise his covenantal love for the Church:

- Jesus gave himself *freely*. He gave his life on the Cross for the sake of us sinners: "No one takes my life from me, but I lay it down on my own. I have power to lay it down, and power to take it up again" (John 10:18).

- Jesus gave himself up *totally* for us. He continues to do so in the Eucharist, his body, blood, soul, and divinity.

- Jesus' love is *faithful*. His love is everlasting, even when we are unfaithful to his will.

- Jesus' love is *fruitful*. His death on the Cross brings new life to those who accept his lordship and repent to receive forgiveness of their sins. The fruit is not only eternal life but also a fruitful life on earth.

In the rite of Matrimony, the engaged couple comes before God and the Church and vow to love one another in a way that reflects the love that Jesus has for the Church. An essential part of the ceremony are the "Questions before the Consent." The celebrant asks the bride and groom a series of questions immediately before they exchange their consent and are married. Embedded in these questions are the four attributes of Jesus' covenantal love to which the bride and groom answer. They take upon themselves to love their spouses freely, totally, faithfully, and fruitfully. Each must answer the items individually.

- *[Name] and [Name], have you come here to enter into Marriage without coercion, freely and wholeheartedly?*
  (freedom of choice and total self-gift)

- *Are you prepared, as you follow the path of Marriage, to love and honor each other for as long as you both shall live?*
  (fidelity to each other)

- *Are you prepared to accept children lovingly from God and to bring them up according to the law of Christ and his Church?*
  (acceptance of children who are the fruit of your love)

The exchange of consent is at the heart of the Catholic wedding ceremony. This is known as the marriage vows.

I (name) take you (name) to be my wife/husband. I promise to be faithful to you in good times and in bad, in sickness and in health, to love you and to honor you all the days of my life.

The wedding rings are blessed and exchanged. The Nuptial Blessing is not only a beautiful prayer but is a blessing on the couple which the priest gives after the Our Father prayer at Mass. The priest faces the couple and raises his anointed hands over them in a gesture invoking the Holy Spirit to come upon them with the sacramental grace of matrimony.

The Nuptial Blessing

> *O God, who by your mighty power created all things out of nothing, and, when you had set in place the beginnings of the universe formed man and woman in your image, making the woman an inseparable helpmate to the man, that they might be no longer two, but one flesh, and taught that what you were pleased to make one must never be divided;*
>
> *O God, who consecrated the bond of Marriage by so great a mystery that in the wedding covenant you foreshadowed the Sacrament of Christ and his Church;*
>
> *O God, by whom woman is joined to man and the companionship they had in the beginning is endowed with the one blessing not forfeited by original sin nor washed away by the flood.*
>
> *Look now with favor on these your servants, joined together in Marriage, who ask to be strengthened by your blessing. Send down on them the grace of the Holy Spirit and pour your love into their hearts, that they may remain faithful in the Marriage covenant.*
>
> *May the grace of love and peace abide in your daughter [name] and let her always follow the example of those holy women whose praises are sung in the Scriptures.*
>
> *May her husband [name] entrust his heart to her, so that, acknowledging her as his equal and his joint heir to the life of grace, he may show her due honor and cherish her always with the love that Christ has for his Church.*

*And now, Lord, we implore you: may these your servants hold fast to
the faith and keep your commandments; made one in the flesh,
may they be blameless in all they do; and with the strength that
comes from the Gospel, may they bear true witness to Christ before
all; may they be blessed with children, and prove themselves,
virtuous parents, who live to see their children's children.*

*And grant that, reaching at last together the fullness of years for
which they hope, they may come to the life of the blessed in the
Kingdom of Heaven. Through Christ, our Lord.*

Amen.

While marital spirituality begins in a Catholic wedding ceremony, the
couple nurtures and lives out that spirituality every day throughout their
marriage. A disciple takes to heart Jesus' command and example, "This is my
commandment: love one another as I love you. No one has greater love than
this, to lay down one's life for one's friends" (John 15:12-13).

Understanding marriage as a vocation, covenant, and sacrament is not merely
an academic view of marriage; these are the very real aspects of the Catholic
vision for marriage. The degree that you and your spouse understand these
concepts and integrate them in your marriage dictates and informs how
you approach it. Your ideas regarding marriage will determine how you
approach your sexual life, financial issues, speech, and attitudes towards your
spouse, conflict resolution, and child-rearing practices. This understanding
of marriage, when integrated in your marriage, provides a solid foundation
for mission within your home and out into the world. The Catholic vision
for marriage does not guarantee perfect marriages or perfect families, but
those who integrate the vision in your relationship work towards making it
a reality for your families.

Sexual Union

The conjugal union of husband and wife is a joy for the unitive and procreative
purposes of marriage. The "marital embrace" of husband and wife is a "good"
of marriage, which means it is a privilege only intended within this vocation.
The unitive purpose calls the husband and wife to develop an open, honest,
and trust-filled relationship—that is, to be "naked" to each other in self-

revelation and self-donation. The sexual union is exclusive for the spouses. Since sexuality affects the whole person in the unity of body and soul, it has a powerful capacity to bond spouses in their affections and love for each other as they experience the joy and pleasure in their union. The procreative purpose calls the husband and wife to be life-giving. Sexual union is the means that God designs for the generation of new human beings. Children are a fruit of marital love, and God calls husbands and wives to become parents to raise and educate children.

The sexual differentiation of male and female allows for compatibility and complementarity between spouses. Their bodies and interior attributes of masculinity and femininity are not merely social constructs; they are realities rooted in the very nature created by God. The male and female bodies have different structures that dictate their functions. The psyche of men and women also differ. If the difference in their bodies is hardware, the difference in the psyche is software. God is spirit, neither male nor female, but he creates human beings as "male and female in his image and likeness" (Genesis 1:27). It is the sexual differentiation between man and woman when they come together in a sexual union that makes it possible for them to become "one flesh." This union is not merely that of bodies but a *communion* of the spouses' innermost being. The one-flesh union makes it possible to bring forth new life.

Couples must discern and be responsible for regulating the size of their families. Natural family planning (NFP) programs teach a couple to understand the natural phases of a woman's fertility cycle so that they may make decisions to achieve or postpone pregnancy as they determine their family size. Because the transmission of life belongs to the vocation of marriage, the practice of NFP is one way that a couple always engages in discerning the will of God for them.

Natural Family Planning

The Church teaches that contraception is immoral and promotes NFP. Why is this? Contraception disregards not only the meaning of human procreation, but it also disrespects the bodies of the spouses.

Marriage is an icon of the Blessed Trinity that reflects the complete exchange of life and love among the three Persons of the one God. Contraception, on the other hand, provides a barrier from the total exchange of persons in the marital act and therefore breaks its sacramentality. NFP, on the other hand, preserves the sacramentality of the marriage because when couples decide to postpone pregnancy by not engaging in the marital act while the wife is fertile, they do not block any exchange of love and life.

Chastity in Marriage

Sexual intimacy is a privilege and joy of marriage that spouses must faithfully guard. Faithfulness in marriage is a constant act of the will to choose the good of the spouse and the marriage bond, including sexual intimacy. Chastity is a virtue required in every vocation. Because sexuality comes into play as an essential part of marriage, spouses need to understand what marital chastity means and how to live this virtue. As the *Catechism* puts it, "Chastity means the successful integration of sexuality within the person, and thus, the inner unity of man in his bodily and spiritual being" (CCC 2337). This means you cannot treat your sexual life as private and separate from other areas of your life. It implies that the bedroom and the sexual act are part of your marital spirituality. As with all virtues, chastity is a habit of choosing the good, and after a while, it becomes easier to choose and do the good. Chastity involves self-control, a restraint made because you put your spouse and marriage before yourself. Like any discipline, it takes practice, growing stronger one choice at a time.

Prudence dictates that spouses establish healthy boundaries with other relationships outside of the marriage to stay on the narrow path and persevere in this vocation. Faithfulness includes making personal choices that will not compromise or endanger yourself or your marriage relationship. Temptations and the inclination to sin (*concupiscence*) are always present in our human condition. Today's cultural and social climate presents many challenges to your marriage vows. Disciples must learn to rely ever more on Jesus and the graces from the sacraments. The power of the Holy Spirit helps you to face and overcome temptations and challenges.

- Francis and Ella serve the Church by giving a talk on "Christian Marriage" for PreCana, a program for engaged couples as part of marriage preparation. In their talk, Ella encourages the engaged young women with advice to fix their eyes only on their husbands. She advises them to watch how they dress so as not to attract sexual advances from other men. Ella also proposes to them to refrain from flirting with other men, as there is no such thing as "harmless" flirting; it can undermine a wife's commitment to her husband. In addition, she advises them to also refrain from responding to any flirtations from other men. She warns them against emotional unfaithfulness, which is more common in women than men, where a woman "nurses" feelings for other men, even without overt actions. This also undermines her faithfulness to her spouse.

- Francis, likewise, addresses the engaged young men with advice to keep their eyes only on their wives. This is challenging because men respond to physical appearance, and our cultural environment highlights arousing physical images. He encourages the men to train themselves in self-control to gain mastery over their senses: much like an athlete trains physically. He advises them to be vigilant by avoiding the near occasions of sin.

- Francis addresses pornography, which is usually more common to men, and he mentions that this addiction impales their freedom to love their wives. He encourages them to repent, seek help, and stamp it out of their marriage.

Besides prayer and the graces from the sacraments, friendship with other Christian couples and being part of a Christian community can help keep husbands and wives accountable to be faithful spouses. When spouses commit sin in any area of their lives, asking God for forgiveness and forgiving each other renews the relationship. Forgiveness and reconciliation allow couples to continue forward without becoming bogged down with anger, resentment, and bitterness. Unforgiveness destroys many marriages because it hardens the heart, disabling its ability to give or receive love. Working on your marriage relationship cannot be assigned to the sidelines of your life. A lasting commitment to your marriage needs the help of the Holy Spirit.

Marital Spirituality Schema

The following Marital Spirituality Schema is a diagram that shows the vital components in the marital spirituality of Catholic couples. Just as an individual disciple strives to have a Christ-centered life, married disciples together strive for a Christ-centered marriage. The Marital Spirituality Schema is similar to the Catholic Discipleship Schema because the essential elements are the same. The difference is that the components refer to activities that a couple does together rather than as individual actions. When done together, these activities help nurture unity and sustain marital spirituality.

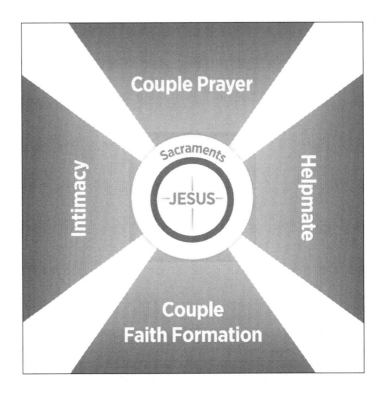

Marital Spirituality Schema

- Jesus is the source of marital spirituality.

- The sacraments provide grace for marital spirituality.

- Prayer brings a couple together before God.

- Study of Scripture and the faith facilitate continued Faith formation.

- Intimacy is the communal life for the couple.

- Being a helpmate is service to the spouse.

These components of marital spirituality bring about conversion to Jesus and spiritual transformation, as well as unity of spouses.

Jesus, the Source of Marital Spirituality

It is Jesus who calls you and your spouse to the vocation of marriage, and he provides what you need to live in this vocation. Every vocation is meant to be lived with Christ because it is through him that transformation in love is possible. To achieve the communion of persons that is God's design for your marriage, you must grow in the self-sacrificial love of Jesus. Marital spirituality is embracing the cross of Jesus so that a new life—the communion of persons with your spouse can spring forth. Husbands and wives who are in communion with Jesus build a bond with each other that is indissoluble.

The Sacraments and Marital Spirituality

The image of the "tree planted beside the water" in the book of Jeremiah is a simple but clear vision for the dynamics involved with Jesus and the sacraments in marital spirituality. The *tree* in this image represents the family tree that your vocation of marriage establishes:

"Blessed is the one who trusts in the Lord, whose hope is the Lord. He is like a tree planted beside the waters that stretches out its roots to the stream: it fears not the heat when it comes; its leaves stay green; in the year of drought it shows no distress, but still bears fruit" (Jeremiah 17:5-8).

The image of the tree planted by the waters reflects the relationship of your family to Jesus and the sacraments of the Church. Just as the tree gets its water directly from the source through the roots, your family receives grace from Jesus and the sacraments through the commitment of the spouses to Jesus and the Church. Marital spirituality serves as the root system of your family tree. As St. Paul tells the church in Ephesus, "That Christ may dwell in your hearts through faith; that you, rooted and grounded in love, may have strength to comprehend with all the holy ones what is the breadth and length and height and depth and to know the love of Christ that surpasses knowledge, so that you may be filled with all the fullness of God" (Ephesians 3:17-19).

Your marital spirituality acting as the root system tapping from the source of grace will equip you to be missionary parents leading the spiritual life of your family and building a domestic church. Roots are opportunistic and will grow to reach sources of water and nutrients, as a tree "stretches its roots to the stream." When the desire and thirst for God lead Catholic disciples to draw even closer to God, you increase your capacity to love God and your family.

The root systems of different trees may have similar functions, but they vary in structure and characteristics. Interestingly, when two trees of the same species grow side by side, they can share root systems that have grafted together as the trees mature. Their connected root systems absorb and transport water and nutrients, not just for one tree but for both! This image characterizes marital spirituality as your growing love for God unites you and your spouse closer to each other.

Couple Prayer

Praying as a couple before God is an essential part of marital spirituality. It is seeking God's presence together. Thanking God together, praising him together, asking together for his help, and together asking for forgiveness is very powerful. Praying the liturgy and sacramental prayers, as well as formal and devotional prayers like the Rosary, or prayers with Scripture present opportunities to be with God. Spontaneous and personal prayers bring intimacy with Christ and with each other. When you and your spouse consistently pray and listen to God together, you can discern what God is doing in your lives and the ways he may be calling you. Anytime you pray together, Jesus is present, "For where two or three are gathered in my name, I am there among them" (Matthew 18:20).

- Every night, Mary and Ryan share the highs and lows of their day. After listening to each other, they come before God and pray for each other. Ryan thanks God specifically for all the good things with which God blessed his wife that day. He also asks God to help her with the challenges she may be facing. Mary, in turn, does the same thing for Ryan. They also bring to God any prayers they have for their children and family, their dreams, desires, aspirations, and challenges.

This is a beautiful way for couples not only to bare their hearts to each other but also bare themselves to God.

Couple Faith Formation

Learning together helps couples be students of the Faith to deepen their marital spirituality. Study of the Scriptures and the Faith helps you continue to grow together in understanding God, the Church, faith, and marriage. The truth revealed from Scripture and Church teachings on marriage will form your minds and hearts as you commit to this relationship. Resources such as the Theology of the Body and NFP are both formative and transformative for a couple. There is an abundance of good resources to enable lifelong faith formation. Many couples include study as part of their relationship by reading Scripture together, listening to or watching Catholic audio and video content, attending conferences, and participating in small groups. Any education on topics that enhances your marriage in spiritual and practical matters will be of great benefit to your relationship.

- Matt and Joy are early risers. Every morning, they read Scripture together and follow a commentary on the passages they read. This naturally leads them to prayer and the sharing of their thoughts and dreams.

- Rob and Marla have a favorite show on a Catholic network that they regularly watch together. What they learn not only deepens their faith but also gets them on their knees to pray for family members who are struggling with particular issues.

Intimacy

Intimacy is the communion-of-persons in marriage that strengthens the bond of marital spirituality. Your friendship with your spouse should enjoy the highest priority among all of your relationships. It takes at least two persons to practice intimacy because it is essentially relational. Intimacy involves an exchange of persons—one spouse entrusts a precious gift, and the other responds with a corresponding gift. In communicating thoughts, feelings, desires, and selves, a spouse becomes vulnerable. The other spouse accesses the "subjective" perspective of the vulnerable spouse. You not only can be in the shoes of your spouse, but in responding appropriately, you indicate that you are walking with your spouse through their experience. Your spouse will know that you care and are trying to understand. This exchange fosters intimacy between husbands and wives.

Married couples enjoy intimacy on several levels: physical, emotional, mental, and spiritual. Without intimacy, couples live in the shallow surface of their relationships, which can lead to loneliness and isolation. Every person has an innate desire to reveal who they are. The deepest need of a person is to be loved, and the most profound desire is to love. Intimacy requires trust and the willingness to make yourself vulnerable to each other.

Fostering intimacy takes time and patience. You can cultivate a relationship that encourages expressing, sharing, and responding. Many adults did not learn interpersonal skills that foster intimacy from their families of origin. Marriage offers the best relationship opportunity to learn and grow in this skill. Couch time could be a simple first step. It is deliberately sitting next to each other and sharing how the day went. Some days, there might not be much to share, but taking the time to sit together becomes a habit. As couples grow in trust, they can begin to share their deeper thoughts, feelings, and desires. Dating on a regular basis can combine fun time together with intimate conversation.

- Tim and Jenna come from very different family backgrounds. Tim comes from a big family where loud talking and disagreements are part of his family's culture. Jenna, on the other hand, grew up with one sister. Many of their early problems arose from the way Tim spoke to her. He was oblivious to the effects that his style of speaking had on Jenna. Eventually, after repeated frustrating encounters, they figured things out and made adjustments to the way they interact. They committed to establishing a regularly scheduled time together as a couple. They now reserve Thursday evenings after the children go to bed to have a time together. This time for themselves helps Tim and Jenna focus on one another intentionally, and it gives them a space to share any pressing matters that lie beyond the superficial.

Helpmate

Being a helpmate to your spouse is a component of marital spirituality that means serving him or her. This service may include helping your spouse in practical ways. More importantly, it is to help your spouse know their dignity as a son or daughter of God.

Challenging them to love and to be accountable to God are also ways of helping your husband or wife. Christian spouses aspire to help each other be holy in preparation for heaven.

- Lisa describes herself as a "feeler." She experiences strong and deep emotions and works through them by talking about them. Nathan describes himself as being "analytic." He works as a computer analyst, and he is a quiet man. When they faced challenges early in their marriage, Nathan would come up with solutions, and Lisa often wondered how he went from A to C without talking through B with her. When she asked him about this, Nathan would think, "I already had this conversation in my head, why should I have it again out loud?" Lisa held him accountable to talk with her so that they could come up with solutions together. Nathan learned to listen to his wife and go through the process of decision-making with her. He also learned to listen when Lisa just needed him to listen to her, even when there were no challenges that needed solutions. Lisa grew to appreciate the stability of her husband when her emotions soared high or dipped low, and she trusted that he thoughtfully considered matters that she brought to him.

Besides being a helpmate to each other, disciples of Jesus have a heart for mission rooted in Jesus' own mission, so the marriage of disciples is missionary at its core. The Lord may also call you as a couple to a particular work in the world or the Church. Couples lend themselves to the scriptural model of Jesus sending his disciples out two-by-two in mission.

- Toby and Lana had become disciples of Jesus before they were Catholic. Their entry into the Church was by way of Natural Family Planning (NFP) and their study of the Theology of the Body. Today, Toby and Lana meet with young couples in their home, both Catholic and non-Catholic, to introduce them to the Theology of the Body. They find the teachings and the ensuing discussions to be an effective means of evangelization.

Jesus and the sacraments are the source of grace to live a Christian marriage. As you and your spouse engage together in prayer, study, intimacy, and being a helpmate to each other, you nourish and fortify your marital spirituality.

Integrated Spiritual Growth

Because a domestic church begins with the marriage of a baptized man and baptized woman, it is essential to understand that the strength of your relationship as husband and wife is only a secondary foundation of the domestic church. Your relationship with Jesus is primary. The following Integrated Spiritual Growth image below shows an integrated personal spiritual life and married spiritual life.

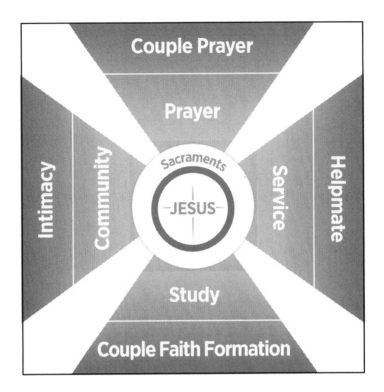

Integrated Spiritual Growth Schema

This image shows the Catholic Discipleship Schema (the inner square) and the Marital Spirituality Schema (outer square) together. As a disciple, you not only continue to have a committed personal relationship with Jesus and the Church, but as a spouse, you integrate your individual spiritual life into the spirituality of your marriage. This is not a separate activity but an *expansion,* both in the width and depth, of your lives as individual disciples. There is no conflict between your faith lives as disciples, and your faith life together as a married couple. It is simply "more" of what has already been established in your life, shared with your spouse.

Like many married persons, you may fear that you have to give up your identity for your marriage to be successful. Rest assured that there is no loss of identity for the disciple of Jesus because your primary identity remains being a son or daughter of God. Fundamental identities are more pronounced in marriage as the dying to self transforms each of you more and more to be like Jesus. The paradox is that, in your marriage, you will become *more of who you are* because marriage strips you of your veneers. Jesus, in obedience to God and in dying for his Bride, the Church, did not lose his identity. He became more distinct and pronounced as the Son of God and Bridegroom to the Church. In your unity of husband and wife, you do not lose your identities as persons; rather, your unity moves you towards freedom from self-preoccupation and self-will to a greater freedom to love. *Gaudium et Spes*, which St. John Paul II helped write, states, "Man cannot fully find himself except through a sincere gift of the self."[5] This is where the vocation of marriage helps you and your spouse grow in holiness and love.

Scripture says, "For the sake of the joy that lay before him, Jesus endured the cross" (Hebrews 12:12). In emulating Jesus, husbands and wives in marital spirituality enter this mystery of death and new life. In living out this rhythm of the Cross and the Resurrection, married disciples have hope to be renewed in every season of life, fortified in every phase of their marriage, and invigorated by hope and joy. In transforming disciples to become more and more like Jesus, the Holy Spirit likewise changes your relationship to conform more and more to the "greatest love story of all time."

Deny Yourself, Pick Up Your Cross, and Follow Jesus

Your discipleship in Christ takes on a deeper and broader scope when you enter the vocation of marriage. Living with a spouse exposes your innermost selves to each other. Your strengths, weaknesses, and character are revealed, not only to your spouse but to yourself. The internal tension inside the married disciple plays out between what you want to do and the demand of love for your spouse. This inner tension is often a real battle. Much of the "conversion opportunity" that marriage presents is overcoming one's selfishness. Pride, competition, ambition, anger, jealousy, strife, and other dark areas of your heart are exposed. These manifest themselves in attitudes, speech, and actions that are offenses against your spouse. When this battle

---

5   Second Vatican Council, *Gaudium et Spes*, 24

wages in the heart, a choice presents itself. You can choose to deny yourself, carry your cross, and follow Jesus for the sake of your spouse and marriage.

In the marital relationship, denying yourself not only means giving up your desires, plans, and control for the sake of your spouse, it also means seeking what is best for him or her. Picking up your cross means not only sacrificing time or comfort for your spouse, it also means being patient, encouraging, and forgiving, especially during difficult times.

To follow Jesus is to imitate him in his free, total, and faithful love for the Church. Jesus leads you to meet the demands of love first before expecting your spouse to meet the demands of love in your marriage. Scripture outlines holy attitudes for husbands and wives who are disciples of Jesus:

> Be subordinate to one another out of reverence for Christ. Wives should be subordinate to their husbands as to the Lord. For the husband is the head of his wife just as Christ is head of the church, he himself the savior of the body. As the church is subordinate to Christ, so wives should be subordinate to their husbands in everything. Husbands, love your wives, even as Christ loved the church and handed himself over for her to sanctify her, cleansing her by the bath of water with the word, that he might present to himself the church in splendor, without spot or wrinkle or any such thing, that she might be holy and without blemish. So also husbands should love their wives as their own bodies. He who loves his wife loves himself. For no one hates his own flesh but rather nourishes and cherishes it, even as Christ does the church, because we are members of his body, 'For this reason, a man shall leave his father and his mother and be joined to his wife, and the two shall become one flesh.' This is a great mystery, but I speak in reference to Christ and the church. In any case, each one of you should love his wife as himself, and the wife should respect her husband (Ephesians 5:21-33).

This exhortation of St. Paul spells out for spouses the ways to deny yourselves, pick up your cross, and follow Jesus. These are not easy, but they are possible with grace and the gifts of the Holy Spirit received in Confirmation: wisdom, understanding, counsel, fortitude, knowledge, piety, and fear of the Lord. These interior gifts can manifest in attitudes and actions for good in your marriage relationship. You can also ask the Holy Spirit for guidance and direction for the choices you make together. A deeper openness to the Holy Spirit will gradually and progressively produce the fruit of love, joy, peace, patience, kindness, generosity, faithfulness, gentleness, and self-control that makes for a beautiful marriage.

The Family Tree

Your family is comprised of individuals and a network of relationships that are dynamic and continually developing. Family members and family life are living elements that need sustained care and protection. It is no wonder that the family is likened to a tree, which grows and bears fruit. A tree has many parts that play different roles to support its life. Without roots, a tree cannot grow. Roots bring the tree stability in the ground as well as water and nutrients from the soil. Marital spirituality serves as the root system of your family tree. It keeps your family firmly grounded, and channels grace, the divine life, to it.

With roots reaching more in-depth into the source of grace, your marriage will produce much fruit, even in times of drought because both you and your spouse "remain in Christ and Christ remains in you" (John 15:4) through the Holy Spirit. As Catholics, approach the sacraments regularly and as a couple, take full advantage of the opportunities to receive the graces that your domestic church requires.

As one cannot see the underground roots of a tree, one cannot observe personal and marital spirituality because they involve the interior life. A healthy root system impacts the life of a tree, while a wholesome marital spirituality influences all of the relationships in your family. Just as the trunk of a tree is readily seen above the ground, a life of faith can be evident in marriage.

Deep roots allow the trunk of the tree to grow in height and width as it matures. The trunk, which constitutes sixty percent of a whole tree, connects the roots to its leafy crown. The crown of a tree is composed of branches, leaves, and fruit. In your family tree, children are fruit that crown your conjugal love and life. Your marital spirituality's influence, effect, and power will be felt in living out your mission as parents. Marital spirituality also bears fruit in the spiritual lives of your children.

TIME TO TALK

1. Do we have a marital spirituality? Have we made an explicit decision to live out the Catholic vision of marriage?

2. What can we do together today to foster unity in our marriage? (Plan a simple but specific action.)

3. Forgive past wrongs, ask God to heal lingering hurts, and renew your commitment to your spouse and your marriage.

PRAYER

Jesus, please bless our marriage to mirror your sacrificial love for the Church. Help us to freely, fully, faithfully, and fruitfully give ourselves to each other. We ask for the grace to grow in unity and fidelity to each other. We give our marriage to you and open it fully to your will, in your precious name we pray, Amen.

Chapter Three

BE MISSIONARY PARENTS

*"Love is the greatest form of evangelization
because it makes an invisible God visible."*

—Jason Evert

Sow seeds.

While in graduate school, Keith and his wife, Kara, had a dream to return with their three children to Keith's family farm in northeast Iowa, which had been in Keith's family for five generations. After graduation, they sold their house and moved to the farm. Fortunately, Keith's father was available to teach them the ropes of farming as they transitioned from city living to farm life. As brand new farmers, Keith and Kara learned much while producing their first crop. For several years, they joyfully worked the land and raised their children. They hope one day their children will take over the farm and continue to keep it in the family.

The same goes with the faith. Parents can only give their children what they have. Husbands and wives must first be disciples of Jesus before they can understand the value of a domestic church, much less have the desire to form their children in the faith. Missionary parents are essential for building a domestic church. Spouses, united in marital spirituality, expand to "make room" for their children. Marital spirituality widens and deepens as they integrate their irreplaceable role as first educators and teachers of the faith to their children. Listening to God's voice, attending to his presence in their shared life, and obeying his will for their marriage moves to a new level to include God's will for their children. A shared life takes the form of a shared mission. For disciple-parents, the family becomes their first mission field.

They become intentional in sowing the seeds of faith, hope, and love in their children, to nurture and protect them so they can mature and bear fruit. With shared roles and tasks, raising a family becomes the most significant work that spouses can do together. When disciple-parents combine Jesus' commission to make disciples and their irreplaceable role as first educators and teachers of the faith to their children, they find a clear path to missionary parenting. This lends itself to an essential design of God that parents bear the most considerable influence on their children's faith life.

A longitudinal study that followed children through their teens and into emerging adulthood has shown the following: "No other conceivable causal influence ... comes remotely close to matching the influence of parents on the religious faith and practices of youth."[6] The model of their parents' faithful relationship with God, a consistent practice of their Catholic Faith, and a healthy, strong marriage will impact and benefit children much more than most parents realize.

Missionary Parents and the Domestic Church

Being missionary parents to their children is the third key relationship essential to a domestic church. Missionary parenting provides leadership to the first faith community. Parents assume the required leadership for their faith community by taking up their irreplaceable roles of first educators and teachers of the faith to their children.

Not only are they biological (or adoptive) parents to their children, but more importantly, they are also spiritual parents to them. As the first faith community, the home is the first place where children hear the Gospel. Whenever there is a proclamation of the Gospel, it requires a response. Missionary parents understand the importance of helping their children have a personal, experiential relationship with Jesus Christ. These experiences lead their children toward accepting the Gospel and responding to God with their full selves—mind, body, and spirit. Family life and the home are the first mission field for Christian parents. In the first faith community of the family, faith in God is the central goal and purpose. The domestic church is where the mission happens as parents become the first educators and teachers of the faith.

First Educators and Teachers of the Faith

The highest calling of Christian parents is to be the first educator and teacher of the faith to their children. This role cannot be delegated to others because the primary qualification is *parental love*, which has an irreplaceable impact on children. For followers of Jesus who are commissioned to go and make disciples, this is a great privilege and joy. The greatest thing parents can offer to their children is not a stable home, food, or college education (although

---

[6]   Smith and Snell, 2009

those are important) but to show them how to love God. The education they aspire for their children is the integration of the faith in all areas of their lives.

The great English theologian G.K. Chesterton offers a perspective on education that helps to capture what kind of education Christian parents provide their children: "Every education teaches a philosophy; if not by dogma then by suggestion, by implication, by atmosphere. Every part of that education has a connection with every other part. If it does not all combine to convey some general view of life, it is not an education at all."[7]

The philosophy that missionary parents desire to impart to their children is rooted in the love of God, others, and oneself. Faith permeating all areas of your children's lives will give meaning and wholeness and promote full human development. Without this foundational philosophy, the various aspects of their lives will float about in different directions. Without God as the foundation, their minds will be susceptible to believing lies, and their hearts will be prone to love what are counterfeits. Concerned with their children's eternal souls, Christian parents hope for their salvation. Missionary parents, therefore, undertake with joy their irreplaceable roles of first educators and teachers of the faith to their children.

So important is your role to teach the faith that St. Thomas Aquinas compares it with the ministry of priests: "Some only propagate and guard spiritual life by a spiritual ministry: this is the role of the sacrament of Orders; others do this for both corporal and spiritual life, and this is brought about by the sacrament of marriage, by which a man and a woman join in order to beget offspring and bring them up to worship God."

There are three components to education: the educator, the environment and methods, and the student. This chapter addresses you, the educator and teacher of the faith. The next chapter is concerned with the environment, which refers to your family life, while the chapter following the next will take a closer look at the child in the domestic church.

Evangelizing Your Children

Your offspring are *persons.* They are one-of-a-kind, unrepeatable individuals with a unity of body and an immortal soul created by God. By receiving and

---

[7] G.K. Chesterton, *The Common Man* (New York: Sheed & Ward, 1950, p.168)

naming each child, parents accept the authority and responsibility for them. It is your responsibility to raise your children to know, love, and serve God. As parents, you are the first proclaimers of the Gospel to your children.

The Catholic Faith is a revealed religion. As such, it requires a proclamation, an announcement. It is necessary to use words to proclaim the Gospel to your children. As St. Paul tells us, "Faith comes from what is heard and what is heard comes through the word of Christ" (Romans 10:17). Parents as first catechists give an explicit sharing of the *kerygma*—the proclamation about the love of God, the passion, death, and resurrection of Jesus for the forgiveness of sins and the power of the Holy Spirit to live the Christian life—to their children. As Pope Paul VI proclaims, "There is no true evangelization if the name, the teaching, the life, the promises, the Kingdom, and the mystery of Jesus of Nazareth, the Son of God are not proclaimed."[8]

Missionary parents proclaim a message that is not yours but is God's Word. You announce it to your children because their souls do not belong to you, they belong to God. In *Lumen Fidei* ("Light of Faith"), Pope Benedict XVI explains that through the act of hearing, faith grows; by becoming familiar with a voice, one begins to know the speaker and a personal relationship develops. When you call your children, they know your voice, they know it is you who is calling them. They respond because of the relationship that exists naturally, and you have a bond built on love and trust. Children become accustomed to hearing the voice of God when parents teach them how to pray. Prayer is a conversation with God, so it necessarily includes both talking and listening. Familiarity with Scripture and the liturgy also familiarizes children with God's voice. Your children will not only come to *know* the voice of God, but they will also learn to *trust* him. From an early age, they will understand their relationship with God as their Father.

Children of God

Christian parents understand that their children are *children of God*. Baptism is the most important day of a child's life from the perspective of eternity. A remembrance of this blessed event will help you consider the seriousness of your role as Christian parents in raising your children.

---

[8]   Pope Paul VI, *Evangelii Nuntiandi*, 22

In the baptismal rite, just before the renunciation of sin and the profession of faith, the celebrant says,

> *"Dear parents and godparents: You have come here to present this child for Baptism. By water and the Holy Spirit, he (she) is to receive the gift of new life from God, who is love. On your part, you must make it your constant care to bring him (her) up in the practice of the faith. See that the divine life which God gives him (her) is kept safe from the poison of sin, to grow always stronger in his (her) heart."*

The celebrant asks parents,

> *"Is it your will that N. should be baptized in the faith of the Church, which we have all professed with you?"*

What was your answer to that question?

After the immersion into or the pouring on of the holy water and the anointing with sacred chrism, the celebrant puts a white garment on the child, saying:

> *"N., you have become a new creation, and have clothed yourself in Christ.*
>
> *See in this white garment the outward sign of your Christian dignity. With your family and friends to help you by word and example, bring that dignity unstained into the everlasting life of heaven."*
>
> *"Amen."*

Finally, the godparents light the baptismal candle from the Easter candle, as the celebrant says:

> *"Parents and godparents, this light is entrusted to you to be kept burning brightly. Christ has enlightened this child of yours. He (she) is to walk always as a child of the light. May he (she) keep the flame of faith alive in his (her) heart. When the Lord comes, may he (she) go out to meet him with all the saints in the heavenly kingdom."*

The celebrant blesses the mother of the child, saying:

> *"God the Father, through his Son, the Virgin Mary's child, has*
> *brought joy to all Christian mothers, as they see the hope of*
> *eternal life shine on their children. May he bless the mother of*
> *this child. She now thanks God for the gift of her child. May*
> *she be one with him (her) in thanking him forever in heaven,*
> *in Christ Jesus our Lord. Amen."*

Then the celebrant blesses the child's father:

> *"God is the giver of all life, human and divine. May he bless*
> *the father of this child. He and his wife will be the first teachers*
> *of their child in the ways of faith. May they be also the best of*
> *teachers, bearing witness to the faith by what they say and do,*
> *in Christ Jesus our Lord. Amen."*

At the beginning of the baptismal rite, the priest traces the Sign of the Cross on your child's forehead and invites you, as parents, and godparents to do the same. This powerful gesture claims your child for Christ as this outward, visible act signifies an interior, spiritual reality. The pouring of (or immersion into) the baptismal waters cleanses your child from original sin. He is plunged with Christ in his death and is raised into a new life. The anointing with chrism incorporates your child into Christ himself, who holds the office of priest, prophet, and king. The baptismal candle, which is lit from the Easter candle, brings the light of Christ into your child's soul. The white garment shows the new dignity of your child as the child of God.

This sacrament truly brings the profound reality of your child's birth in the Spirit, and an indelible mark begins a life of discipleship. Your child belongs to Christ because Jesus paid a high price—his very life—for him.

When you brought your child to the Church for baptism, you agreed to raise him in the new life with Christ. You must follow through on your promise because your child is now a child of God. Through baptism, your child has a relationship with God—even if an infant cannot intentionally contribute to his relationship with him. God actively contributes to the relationship.

This is like your child's relationship with grandparents. The grandparent-grandchild status forms, regardless of whether there is an active contribution on the part of the child to the nurturing of this relationship. In their child's relationship both with God and his grandparents, you, as parents, play an essential role in introducing and supporting those relationships as your child grows. Unlike relationships with grandparents, though, your child's relationship with God is readily and directly accessible at whatever age. Your child can actively love God and respond to God's love. The ordinary way for children to first know, love, and serve God is through the parents and their first faith community.

Intentionally building a domestic church will help you to pursue what you set out to aspire when you brought your child for Baptism. The training in love that you strive to implement at home will require not only your unity as husband and wife but also trust in God, who will provide the grace necessary for this high calling.

Fundamental Concepts of a Person

Your responsibility to educate and teach the faith to a child of God requires an understanding of the value of a *person*. Every philosophy, spirituality, religion, movement, or educational process offers fundamentals based on how it regards the human person, God, and the purpose of life. How does Hinduism see the person, God, and life? Islam? The American educational system? How does feminism regard the human person, God, and life? What about modern psychology or consumerism? The value of your child as a person, the reality of God, and the meaning of life underline how you educate and teach the faith to your children.

Scripture presents the human person as a being created by God in his image and likeness. The Catholic Faith teaches that God is a personal and loving communion of Persons, a God who is not distant but lives in each baptized Christian. The Christian life, then, is a journey toward union with God through a transformation in love with the help of grace. The goal is heaven. These fundamental concepts are truths revealed by God through the Sacred Scripture and Sacred Tradition. In educating your child, missionary parents embrace these Christian perspectives on the infinite value of a person, a loving God and a purposeful life.

Two considerations shed light on the view of a person that will help in your role as educator and teacher: 1) the three relationships into which a child is born, and 2) core Catholic values.

There are three relationships into which each child is born that are affected by our fallen human nature and that only Jesus can restore to their original design:

1. *Relationship with God.* Every person has a relationship with God because God created each person.

2. *Relationship with others.* Every person enters the world in a relationship with parents or some other adult who provides the child's basic needs. The family is the first community that the person will experience.

3. *Relationship with oneself.* Every person will begin to form a value of himself by the way others treat him.

Accordingly, the core of Catholic values is concerned with these three relationships. A person made in the *image and likeness of God* ...

> ... has *inherent dignity* and a *right to life.*

> ... is *rational* and has *free will*, which is the ability to initiate and control his or her actions.

> ... is a *social being* with a right to participate in community of which the family is the first community.

> ... has a natural inclination to *seek knowledge* and to *discover truth*, which is ultimately directed to God. Only in God can a person find true happiness.

The Great Commandment becomes not an arbitrary directive but a statement about the nature of the human person as created by God.

> When the Pharisees heard that he had silenced the Sadducees, they gathered together, and one of them, a scholar of the law tested him by asking, "Teacher, which commandment in the law is the greatest?" He said to him, "You shall love the Lord, your God, with all your heart, with all your soul, and with all your mind. This is the greatest and the first commandment. The second is like it: You shall love your neighbor as yourself. The whole law and the prophets depend on these two commandments (Matthew 22: 34-40).

In considering the three relationships and core Catholic values, your role becomes more evident as to what the goals are for teaching the faith to your children.

The Parent-Child Relationship

A new father once commented, referring to his newborn son, "I cannot believe how such a small thing who cannot do anything can change me!" It is precisely the helplessness of an infant that calls forth parents to provide and protect their child. There is a love that parents experience for their child that they never experienced before nor understand its power over them. This parental love, however, gives missionary parents a taste of the great love, compassion, and mercy that God has for all. All human fatherhood and motherhood are rooted in the fatherhood of God. Parents can truly experience, to a small extent, the love of God for his children.

As parents grow in love and responsibility, "Children contribute to the growth in holiness of their parents" (CCC 2227). God gives parents authority over their children. Therefore, parents are accountable to God on how they exercise this authority with their children. There are two extreme approaches that a parent should avoid:

1. *Authoritarian.* In this approach, a parent mistakenly believes the aim of parenting is to control children's behavior rather than to help them learn and grow in self-control and determine their behavior.

2. *Yielding.* Here, a parent thinks it is "all about the child," and the aim of parenting is to let the child's desires, emotions, and thoughts determine the parent's decisions.

Both are disrespectful of the parent-child relationship. In the authoritarian approach, the parents abuse their authority, while in the yielding approach, parents hand over to the child the responsibility that properly belongs to them as parents. On significant issues, parents must take the lead. Depending on the age and maturity of the child, parents can allow their children to contribute their input on matters. This is where having a domestic church brings clarity. A parent can determine how decisions align with the fundamental values that have been established for the family.

There is a mutual love that grows between parents and the child. Scripture gives this guideline for parent-child relationships: "Children, obey your parents in the Lord, for this is right. Honor your father and mother" Ephesians (6:1-2). This is the first commandment with a promise, "so that it may go well with you and that you may have a long life on earth. Fathers, do not provoke your children to anger but bring them up with the training and instruction of the Lord" (Ephesians 6:4).

This Scripture verse is concerned with the responsibilities of children and parents to one another. The responsibility of children to parents will be discussed in another chapter. This chapter on being missionary parents is concerned with the second part of the verse. It directs fathers, but you may consider it as a direction for parents. "Bring them up with the training and instruction of the Lord"—the *training* part here concerns the training of the will, and the *instruction* part has to do with the formation of the mind. Parents transmit the truths of the faith, instill Christian values, impart knowledge, and share understanding about virtues. These will help form the child's mind and heart. The knowledge has to be accompanied by the training of the will so that the child will be able to direct himself to act, decide, and move towards the good. Parents provide and coach their child in the training of the will through daily family life.

The Will

Because of their inherent dignity, children need training in how to exercise their free will. In this regard, parents provide training, not by providing a multitude of options for every choice but by engaging their children. The use of the will is not merely asking your child's preference on a matter at hand. It entails your child making a choice and initiating an action directed by his interior determination. This training and engagement happen in the small daily interactions of family life. The repeated choosing and habitual acting in goodness form virtue and character.

When children have clear goals, many opportunities to exercise their will, and an expectation to act rightly, they move their will to do so. Many times, a child does not even need the customary "pat on the back" because the little daily sense of accomplishment serves as a personal reward. The daily routines of school work, extracurricular activities, relationships, and family life all can be opportunities to help your children grow in virtue and training of their will.

The will plays a vital role in a Christian's life, for it is by the will that one chooses to love, which is manifested in one's actions. The will has the dual job of obeying God and governing the self. The formation and strengthening of the will give members of the family the capacity to make wise and firm choices even in the face of opposition, temptation, and difficulty. A weak will can know all about the good and true, but it will not be free to act in love, to give away the self, and to deny itself. Instruction in virtuous conduct and training the will are interdependent. As a child learns something, he can direct his will to act on it. When he directs his will to work on something, he learns more personally. The knowledge becomes integrated into his person. Parents can take full advantage of all the opportunities to teach and train if there is an overarching plan for each child. A plan brings all the seemingly separate areas of family life into an integrated whole.

Missionary Parenting Schema

The following Missionary Parenting Schema is a diagram that reflects the essential components in the irreplaceable role of first educators and teachers of the faith to your children. Missionary parents take up roles of leadership in various areas of the family's life that together, form the domestic church.

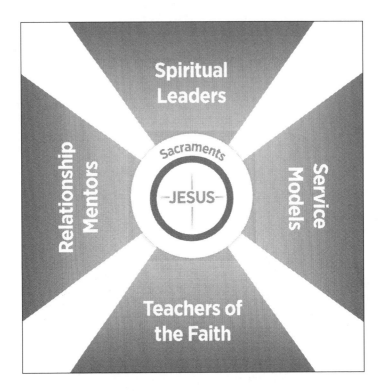

Missionary Parenting Schema

- The relationship of parents with Jesus is the center of missionary parenting.

- The sacraments are central to the life of parenting.

- Parents choose to be the spiritual leaders of their families.

- Parents opt to be the teachers of the Faith to their children.

- Parents become relationship mentors of their children.

- Parents decide to be models of service to their children.

These components in missionary parenting help parents to be deliberate in the education of their children.

Jesus Is at the Center of Missionary Parenting

Jesus, the Good Shepherd, gives parents the capacity to become loving shepherds to their children. Your vocation that started as a simple call expands to include responsibilities for children of God. Jesus provides you with a shepherd's heart for your children. You grow in your ability to lead, feed, care for, bind their wounds, to seek them when lost, and to protect them. Like the Good Shepherd, you lay your life down for them. Jesus calls each of your children by name. He enjoins parents, "Let the children come to me, and do not prevent them; for the kingdom of heaven belongs to such as these" (Matthew 19:14).

The Sacraments and Missionary Parenting

As missionary parents look to the Church and the sacraments for graces to live out your Christian life, you also look to the Church to provide these same spiritual encounters to your children. As the *Catechism* teaches, "The parish is the Eucharistic community and the heart of liturgical life of Christian families. It is a privileged place for the catechesis of parents and children" (CCC 2226). A family is a unit of the local parish and the universal Church. Receiving the sacraments incorporates your children into Jesus and his Body, the Church, when they receive them. You accompany and teach your children as they prepare for the sacraments of initiation. When Catholic parents raise their children in the Faith, it is the natural way for the Church to grow.

In the Missionary Parenting Schema, the components represent the roles that parents assume in the domestic church.

Spiritual Leaders

As spiritual leaders, your role in your family is irreplaceable; no one else can fill this role but you. It is natural for children to look to their parents for guidance and leadership. This natural respect applies to the spiritual life as well: "Parents should initiate their children at an early age into the mysteries of the Faith and associate them from their earliest years to the life of the Church" (CCC 2225). The most important spiritual practice that you can teach your children is *prayer.* Prayer demonstrates to children that God is not only present in your lives but that you also have a loving relationship with him. Help your children discover and enjoy God's presence. He has been with them from the first moment of their lives. In prayer, show your children how they can respond to the tender love God has for each of them—in other words, how they can love God. Children understand relationships, and they can recognize love at any age. Spiritual leadership means praying with and for your children, and leading the family in prayer.

- Besides prayers before meals, Dirk and Kate lead their children in prayer every night before bedtime. They all gather together on their knees. One by one, each child makes spontaneous prayers. Even their one-year-old daughter stays still and listens to her family's prayers, making sounds when they tell her it is her turn to pray.

- Charles had the practice of making a holy hour of Eucharistic adoration on Friday evenings at seven o'clock. When his children grew to be toddlers, his wife and children joined him. At first, the little ones slept in the pews. As they grew, they were able to stay awake longer, so the entire family began to pray the Rosary together during part of their holy hour. Later, in middle school, they started bringing holy books to read. Now, as high schoolers, they have added Bible reading to their adoration.

Another critical piece of spiritual leadership for parents is helping your children know the Scriptures as God's word. The Bible is the narrative of the Kingdom of God from beginning to end, in which God and his people are the main actors. Central in the Scriptures is Jesus Christ, the beginning and end of the faith, the Way the Truth and the Life. Baptism brings children into the New Covenant with God and knowing the Scriptures will familiarize and orient them in this covenant. Taking the children to Mass and the sacrament of Reconciliation are other essential actions of spiritual leadership. Who else will teach these primary Christian pursuits to your children? Where else will the doors to the spiritual life open for them? How else will they know the definition of love than hearing how Jesus laid down His life for them?

- Because Luke and Julie live outside of town with their family, it takes about twenty minutes to get to their parish church for Sunday Mass. In the car on the way to church, Julie reads the first and second readings, as well as the Gospel, for that particular Sunday. This helps to prepare their children to listen more attentively to the readings at Mass.

Teachers of the Faith

The home becomes a school where you teach your children about love, virtue, faith, and the teachings of the Church. Because you, as missionary parents, are students engaged in lifelong faith formation, you are ready to be the first and best teachers of the faith. Passing along the faith includes teaching the revealed truths, both implicitly and explicitly. As parents, you educate your children *implicitly* by your choices and decisions. You teach them *explicitly* by explaining to them the reasons why you make choices and decisions informed by your faith. Always consider the age and maturity of children as you help them integrate the teachings of the Faith. Be straightforward and clear in imparting knowledge about the faith in its fullness, and be ready to be compassionate and kind when presenting moral teachings based on love.

- When the children were very young, Dan read stories to them after supper. As they got older, he started to do a family devotional that included a Bible verse, a story that children could relate to, and a discussion question for the children to answer to start a discussion. When the children were in middle school, the family read the *YouCat* together (which is the *Catechism of the Catholic Church* for youth presented in a question and answer format). Each family member would read aloud one question and answer until everyone had their turn.

Relationship Mentors

By your example and instruction, you take on the role of mentors in loving relationships. It is important to affirm each of your children as a unique, unrepeatable *person*. This begins with understanding each child's inherent value, unique qualities, and character. Expressing these to each of your children, both verbally and non-verbally, is a significant way to affirm their value. Because the family is the first place one experiences Christian life, your relationship with your children helps to form their understanding of who they are. Your relationship also provides them with a base for understanding loving relationships. It is in relationships that they will learn virtue.

Virtue plays an important role in one's relationships with others. Virtue is none other than the practice of habitually choosing and doing the good. It is in the family that parents instill values, practice virtue, and form the home's moral compass. As the *Catechism* puts it, "The home is well-suited for the education of virtues. This requires an apprenticeship in self-denial, sound judgment, and self- mastery—the preconditions for true freedom" (CCC 2223). The consistent practice of loving behavior helps members of the family to order their powers and appetites such that positive response becomes easier as charity becomes a habit. To grow in virtue significantly forms the child's moral character.

Moral formation becomes effective when it is based on relationships rather than a list of rules. Moral formation happens when living in a community because it is concerned with the good of the self and others. For children (and adults), morality makes sense when it is based on love and framed in the context of a love relationship with God and others. Another strong basis for moral formation is instilling a sense of solidarity with everyone. Being aware of their own faults and weaknesses inspires children to have compassion for others. Discipline, forgiveness, kindness, self-control, and honesty are characteristic of Christian life that help to form their consciences—which, in turn, will inform their decisions throughout their lives. Clear and explicit teaching is vital for the formation of conscience, followed by an exhortation to act.

There are three dimensions in moral formation:

1. *Preparing the intellect.* That is, having an understanding of moral principles.

2. *Preparing the heart.* This involves growing in one's love for God, as well as one's respect for others.

3. *Preparing the will.* Instilling the self-discipline to carry out the actions that the mind and heart know are right.

These three dimensions of moral formation can be illustrated by teens learning to drive. First, they learn the essential principles and rules of driving in a classroom. Then, they learn to accept and respect these rules. Finally, they get behind the wheel for some "on the road" instruction and practice with a driver education teacher. Only then can they operate a car in traffic. Children need instruction, acceptance, and practice to learn how to drive because driving involves their whole person. Driving a car is a skill, while moral formation involves one's interior self. The process of learning and integrating something new is the same, though. Effective learning happens when the intellect, heart, and will (and body) are engaged. This process holds true for children of all ages.

Reading stories with clear moral lessons early on in childhood helps form a child's moral imagination. Providing immediate feedback on the choices that your children make gives them guidance on their decision-making and provides them with standards for making good choices.

- Joel and Lynn and their children receive the sacrament of Reconciliation once a month. Besides having their sins forgiven and receiving the sacramental grace to avoid future sins, Lynn says that it improves their family relationships. Having to ask forgiveness from God for their sins, they must also forgive the offenses of their family members against them. It is like unclogging the pipes, so that the water can run through unimpeded. The penance they receive from the priest usually involves an act of charity for a family member, so each one has an opportunity to practice charity intentionally. (After confession, they have a tradition of getting ice cream to celebrate in joy that their souls are now "white as snow.")

Disciple-parents also model to their children how to be members of a Christian community. Children watch you and your relationships with others. You may be part of a men's or women's group or a community of families in your parish. The Christian community plays a vital role for individuals and couples as you offer your gifts to the community and also receive from it. The community becomes an invaluable resource when individual struggles and spousal challenges arise because you have Christian brothers and sisters who are willing to support you and pray for you.

Service Models

As the *Catechism* notes, parents model service to children by serving each other and the family: "The home is the natural environment for initiating a human being into solidarity and communal responsibilities" (CCC 2224). Parents teach children service by letting them contribute to the care of the home and the family by age-appropriate chores. Through service, not only are gifts discovered, developed, and used for the family, but the interdependency and mutual responsibility for each family member grows.

With your varied gifts, you may also be called to serve outside of the home. Parents model participation in the greater family of God to work for the common good. You can include your children in this work, modeling for them Christian charity and the generous use of your gifts for the good of others.

- Grace likes to cook, so she prepares a meal for families who have a newborn child. She involves her daughters by asking them to make dessert for the family.

- John has been going every Saturday morning to the men's emergency housing in the city. He gathers the homeless men to read a short excerpt from the Bible, and he reads a short devotional reflection on the passage. Then open sharing occurs to allow the men to reflect on the meaning and to share personal experiences. They close with prayer and then go to a local restaurant for breakfast. His teenage son has attended the meeting since he was three. At first, his son was just interested in the breakfast, but as he grew older, he became more engaged in the discussion and prayer. In high school, his son continued to go with John every Saturday morning, and when he got a job bagging at the supermarket, he began to contribute money to buy breakfast for the men as part of his tithing.

A critical part of the mission of missionary parents is to help your children discover their vocation, the particular way that God is calling them to participate in his work. In a way, raising them means equipping and forming them to be able to respond freely and fully to the specific call that the Lord has for them. Their vocation is God's call in their life for their sanctification, service to the Church, and to further God's kingdom on earth.

Commit to Educate

Educators are leaders, not just managers. Leaders lead people. Managers, on the other hand, administer and control resources and activities. You do need to manage the resources and activities of your family to provide proper care for your children. As an educator, however, you must commit to guiding the minds and hearts of your children. More significant than the plans, strategies, structures, and environments for your family, you as the educator carry the most impact. All of the externals you provide to your family are only expressions of your internal attitudes, dispositions, and priorities as the educator. As a disciple, remain open to the work of the Holy Spirit to transform you interiorly to expand your capacity to love your children and teach them.

Educators continue to be students as they teach. The virtue of humility enables you to learn and grow along with your children. A missionary parent remains teachable and looks to the Holy Spirit as Teacher. There will be many mistakes, back-peddling, and adjustments, but it is your commitment and attitude that your children observe. You have a limited window of time (eighteen years) to form, teach, and raise your children. Like Jesus' commitment to develop and teach his disciples and establish the Church (he did it in three years), you commit to disciple your children and build your domestic church.

Deny Yourself, Pick up Your Cross, and Follow Jesus

Your discipleship in Christ becomes much more involved when your marital relationship bears the fruit of children. Your vocation is like a small spring that grows and swells into a river as water from other sources joins its flow. Each child brings a new pattern to family relationships. Children will bring out the best—as well as the worst—in you. Without a commitment to be the first educators and teachers of the faith to your family, you will continuously experience the tension between choosing what you want to do and the demands of loving your children and family. You will be tempted to let outside educators, coaches, catechists, caregivers, the media, and others form your children's hearts and minds. The Church provides Catholics with light on matters of faith and morals, many of which are countercultural. Who will transmit these to your children? The tension can also be felt because of ambition, job demands, recreational activities, other relationships that tempt you to be distant from your family life or disengaged in your relationships with your spouse and children. Sometimes, even ministries, charities, and work for the Church tempt you to make them priorities over your family relationships. Who will educate and teach your children?

The proper spiritual and moral formation of your children rests in your hands because the gift of faith you have received, you must now give. It is here where you die to yourself, carry your cross, and follow Jesus for the sake of your children. Denying yourself means letting go of your personal comforts, desires, and plans so you can give yourself to your family. Picking up your cross means engaging in your irreplaceable role as the first educator and teacher of the faith to your children. To follow Jesus is to develop the heart of the Good Shepherd, who leads the sheep out to pasture and leads them into the sheepfold, their home. When you die to yourself, new life in Christ follows. God will provide you the grace to renew your strength to live the commitment.

Sow Bountifully

Springtime in Iowa has farmers earnestly watching the weather to determine the right time to plant their corn, when the soil is warm enough. One of our friends, Ray, who grows corn on his four-hundred-acre family farm, says, "I consider it a miracle when I plant seeds in the ground, they germinate, grow into stalks, develop ears of corn—and have several kernels on one cob!" The farmer plants the seed corn and oversees its growth until harvest time. In Iowa, farmers plant corn on 13.5 million acres of land. That translates to a lot of grain and hours of planting in the spring. For travelers trekking through Iowa, hundreds of miles of cornfields may seem boring. For those of us who live here, though, the thick landscape of rows and rows of tall green corn stalks is a picture of bounty.

Like the farmer, missionary parents are deliberate in sowing seeds of faith, hope, and love into your children's minds and hearts. As St. Paul tells us, "Whoever sows sparingly will also reap sparingly, and whoever sows bountifully will also reap bountifully" (2 Corinthians 9:6). *Sparingly* means giving but holding back, thinking not how much you can offer but how much to keep to yourself. In educating children, this amounts to a minimal investment of time and effort. *Bountifully* means giving from the heart with a desire to share. In teaching your children, you invest time and effort to form their minds and hearts through your words and actions.

Missionary parents become more and more thankful to God as they increasingly understand God's generosity when he did not spare his only Son. They progressively grow in generosity also as they consider that everything is a gift from God: "Moreover, God is able to make every grace abundant for you, so that in all things, always having all you need, you may have an abundance for every good work … the one who supplies seed to the sower and bread for food will supply and multiply your seed and increase the harvest of your righteousness" (2 Corinthians 9:8,10).

TIME TO TALK

1. Do we have a desire to build our family as a domestic church? Do we have a vision for our family?

2. What steps can we take today towards becoming the first and best educators and teachers of the Faith to our children?

3. How can we be more intentional in teaching our children to pray?

PRAYER

Father in heaven, thank you for the gift of fatherhood and motherhood. Help us to be the first and best educators of the Faith to our children. We desire that each of our children know you personally and intimately, now and throughout their lives. Give us wisdom, in Jesus' name, Amen.

Chapter Four

ESTABLISH A FAMILY SPIRITUALITY

*"The spirituality of family love is made up of thousands of
small but real gestures. In that variety of gifts and encounters
which deepen communion, God has his dwelling place."*

—Pope Francis

Provide Fertile Soil.

Whenever a speaker says the word *dirt* around us, our children look at us like someone just said a bad word. In our family, we do not refer to soil as dirt. We use the word *soil* to provide significance and value to the material underfoot. I (Bob) am a soil scientist, teaching and doing basic research on soil and collaborating with several soil scientists around the world on various soil investigations. I know that soil is undervalued and does not receive the respect it deserves as the very foundation of the food chain.

They call our soil "the black gold of Iowa" to highlight its high fertility for crop growth. The build-up of decomposed organic material for centuries formed the black topsoil of Iowa. Fertile soil contains the essential nutrients for plant growth. Much like soil is to plants, the family is the privileged place ordained by God where human beings begin life, grow, and develop. Missionary parents not only sow seeds of faith, hope, and love, but they also prepare fertile soil so that those seeds may germinate, take root, and grow. Family life presents an environment that fosters authentic growth and development. When there is an explicit agreement between husband and wife to raise their children Catholic, parents establish a family spirituality, which is the substructure for an environment centered on faith. Family life becomes fertile soil that will bear fruit: "But those sown on rich soil are the ones who hear the word and accept it and bear fruit thirty and sixty and a hundredfold" (Mark 4:20).

Family Spirituality and the Domestic Church

Family spirituality, Christ-centered relationships shared among family members, is the fourth key essential to a domestic church that unites members of the family into a faith community. Faith in God is both explicit and expressed in the family. In the early church, households became the first communities that lived the way of Christ. As the *Catechism* says, "From the beginning, the core of the Church was often constituted by those who had become believers together with all their household. When they converted, they desired that 'their whole household' should also be saved. These families who became believers were islands of Christian life in an unbelieving world" (CCC 1655). In the early Church, the evangelization of individuals happened in the context of a family community. Their faith formed a united household that lived in a particular way, different from those around them. Family spirituality allows family members to accompany each other on the journey rather than travel as individuals. Everyone needs encouragement, companionship, protection, and food for the journey. Family spirituality fosters the *communion of persons,* which is how the Church defines family.

We mentioned in Chapter Three that any education process has three aspects: the educator, the environment or methods, and the student or child. Here, we will briefly present the role of the environment in the education of your child.

Home Environment

The home environment is essential to missionary parents because it affords you the space for your mission, the education of your children. Their education requires a nurturing environment for their full human development. Your family life speaks to your children's minds and hearts even without words. It carries messages that they understand and internalize. As Pope Paul VI says, "Modern man listens more willingly to witnesses than to teachers, and if he does listen to teachers, it is because they are witnesses."[9] More than anything you provide your children, it is your Christian witness that will speak to their minds and hearts. Children perceive intangibles even without understanding them. Missionary parents can maximize the influence of the environment on their children's education by understanding its impact and plan accordingly.

The family is the first and most significant environment that your children experience. Children have great need and capacity for relationships as they depend on others for their basic needs. From a very early age, they absorb the culture of this environment by imitating family members' actions and reactions. Trust is formed as your child experiences confidence in relationships.

The home is the place where the children learn their inherent value as a person. This value is not contingent on what they do, the gifts and talents they have, or how they look. A child forms her self-image and self-worth in no small part

---

[9] *Evangelii Nuntiandi,* 41

by the way she perceives it through the primary relationships in the family. Respect, positive regard, and affection convey to children value and worth.

When faith in God holds a central place in the family, children become aware of their relationship with God—and this opens up for them a way to engage intentionally with him. Family spirituality fosters many opportunities for your children to relate to God during their years of growth and development at home.

Family spirituality serves as the glue that binds family members into a domestic church. It encompasses the whole life of the family, both its inner and exterior life, because the spiritual life bears fruit that will be evident in the decisions and actions of each family member. A family spirituality formed by the presence of God and the communion of persons represents the crown of your family tree.

Crown of Your Family Tree

When spouses become one flesh, they are bound to each other. Their communion becomes a home for their children. Home is, at the same time, a place for resting and an environment for becoming. It provides a safe place for being and yet still growing. Family members can experience mercy, compassion, support, and encouragement from one another. Every person needs a home to facilitate and support wholesome human progress.

Home corresponds to the crown of your family tree that features branches that grow out from the main trunk and supports the leaves and fruit. Your family life emerges from your marriage relationship and encompasses all its members, relationships, and activities. The branches, leaves, and fruit depend on the trunk and roots for water and nutrients from the soil.

Your marital spirituality overflows to form a family spirituality. Whereas leaves catch sunlight for energy for the plant, family relationships animate family life. The fruit is the means for a tree to reproduce itself like children are the means for transmission of human life. Just as a tree is one organism, your family is one community.

Your home houses your family in a community. It is not only a place of relationships with God, others, and the self, but it is also the place for the first experience of communal life for the children. Family spirituality facilitates the development of your family's communal life. This communal life strengthens the domestic church as it serves as an apprenticeship to be active members of society and the communal life of the greater Church.

The Communal Life

The communal life is the shared life of the family that forms it into a single community. The Catholic understanding of family as a communion of persons and the idea of intentional community help parents build a communal life for their family. The recognition of the social nature of persons made to live with others motivates parents to pursue forming an intentional community, which has leaders and a purpose. In the family, parents are the leaders. Their faith guides them in raising their children and transmitting the faith. The purposes of the community are to serve life and help its members grow in love. Additionally, a faith community has the purpose of handing down the faith.

There are two considerations to incorporate into the intentional communal life of the family:

1. *Stewardship*: the management of shared resources for which a family is responsible.

2. *Catholic social values*: every society has a set of values that members of that society understand that allow them to have an orderly society. The Spartans, for example, placed high social value on an individual's strength, so that they could be fierce soldiers. For your family as a faith community, faith in God should be of the highest value. To form a communal life, learning and applying Catholic social values provide helpful guidelines.

Stewardship

Stewardship means the management of resources for the common good and the development of its members. Stewardship comes from sincere gratitude to God for all the blessings that disciples consider as gifts from him. This comes into play in the stewardship of a family's time, talents, and treasure. Good stewardship, as modeled by parents, becomes a way of life for every member of the family.

- Good stewardship of a family's *time* involves balancing the time of each member and of the family as a community. Family members set aside time for prayer, play, work, and rest. Down time and quiet time are essential for family members to be refreshed and have time to think. Schedules for waking up, mealtimes, and bedtimes give children structure and support healthy living. Time management, as taught and modeled by parents, is a skill that children learn.

> ▷ Besides writing in appointments and activities in a family calendar, a mom often announced to her young children her plans for the day. This prepared her children for what to expect that day. As they got older, her children began the habit of loosely planning their day along with fixed schedules.

- Good stewardship of *talents* involves balancing individual development of gifts, such as sports, music, and hobbies, and using abilities in family service, such as washing dishes or cleaning.

> ▷ Devon enjoys playing the piano and diligently practices every day. When his parents invite friends or family over for dinner or a visit, they often ask Devon to play the piano for their guests.

- Good stewardship of *treasure* means a wise distribution of financial resources, balancing spending, saving money for future needs, tithing to the parish, or donating to a worthy cause.

> ▷ Danny and Kim devised a plan to teach their children the value of money by making a list of jobs around the house and paying them to do them. (These are apart from their normal chores.) They pay their children at the end of each weak and teach them to give ten percent to the parish, put forty-five percent in a savings jar, and let them spend the remaining forty-five percent on anything they choose.

Parents lead and model stewardship to their children and encourage their children to make decisions to be good stewards of their time, talents, and treasure.

Catholic Social Values

The Catholic Church has a vibrant social teaching tradition. Although the family is the smallest unit of society, understanding these social values means understanding the nature of each family member as a social being and shaping each to be responsible members of a community:

1. *Human life is sacred, and the dignity of the human person is foundational to a moral vision.* Respect for each member of the family is fundamental in all relationships. The child contributes to the community by his very presence.

2. *Call to family, community, and participation.* Every family member should be given the opportunity for these in the family.

3. *Rights and responsibilities.* Because of their human dignity, family members have rights, privileges, and responsibilities in being part of the family. This is the full engagement of the whole person in the life of the family.

4. *Option for the poor and vulnerable.* Parents teach family members to minister to the needs of the most vulnerable members of the family, such as elderly members, infants, children with disabilities, or other members when they are sick or experiencing difficulties.

5. *The dignity of work and the rights of workers.* Work is a participation in the life of the family. Everyone's contribution must be respected.

6. *Solidarity.* The love for other members of the family leads each one to work for peace and extend compassion for one another.

7. *Care for God's creation.* Family members learn the care of self, pets, plants, the environment, and nature in general.

Respected as individuals, family members orient themselves in the communal life of the family. All members of the family care and look after each other's needs because each person has value. There is one activity that is the epitome of family communal life, eating meals together.

Family Meals

A family who shares a meal around a table is a picture of universal, human, and communal experience. Unlike animals, for humans, eating is not merely a necessity to support biological life. Eating together as a family is a significant social activity that crosses all cultures. It remains a communal activity that strengthens the family. Many research support the positive effects of eating meals together as a family on children's academic performance. The effect lies in having a sense of belonging and emotional stability that eating as a family instills. Many factors today encroach on family dinner time, and missionary parents must resist these factors. More and more, you and your children experience impersonal interactions daily on social media and the Internet as a whole. Sitting at the dinner table is a meaningful interaction that makes family members more human because they can look into each other's eyes and recognize each other's value.

Busy parents must make an effort to safeguard family dinner time so that members can connect after a day of being apart. It will surprise tired parents that prayer and meaningful conversations with family members provide not only rest but refreshment from the day's often frenzied schedule. Dinner time is a communal activity that, when done regularly, connects family members consistently.

- When the Duncan family gathers for dinner every evening, each person shares a high point and a low point of their day.

The communal life provides an education for family members to consider the needs of the whole community, which many times, calls individuals to sacrifice their needs and desires. Family life calls each one to participate and contribute to sustaining a shared life. The reality reflected by communal life is that every person makes a difference and is needed for the life of the community. The sense of belonging does not come about in having the same last name, but it emerges from meaningful participation in a community. Belonging is working side-by-side with family members towards a common life. This is a training ground not only for loving others, but it also prepares children for full Christian discipleship. Family spirituality dynamically integrates faith in all areas of family life, including the communal life.

- John and Ruth encourage their children to make sacrifices by asking them, "Who is willing to make a sacrifice?" They ask this, in particular, when their children are fighting over one thing or something unpleasant needs to be done.

Family Spirituality Schema

The Family Spirituality Schema is a diagram that shows the essential components in the development of your family as a faith community. The components are areas of family life that when developed, serve as the fertile soil that is optimal for human growth and development. They facilitate and promote loving relationships between and among family members.

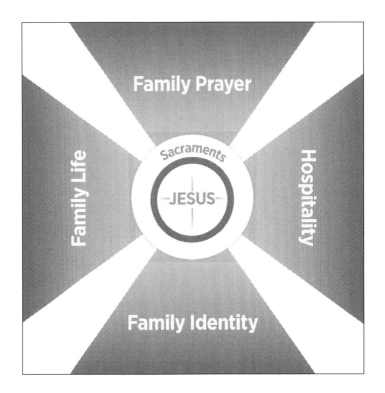

Family Spirituality Schema

- The family is centered on Jesus.

- The sacraments are central to the life of the family.

- Family prayer is a regular practice in the first faith community.

- Family identity brings a sense of cohesiveness and belonging.

- Family life is the shared life of all members of the family.

- Hospitality opens the family to others.

These components of family spirituality bring about family members into a community.

Jesus at the Center of the Family

Jesus refers to himself as the true Vine and to his followers as the branches. This image demonstrates the connectivity of branches (us) to the vine (Jesus), and the branches to each other in the vine. The sap that runs through the whole vine is its inner life, distributed to all of its parts. Jesus tells his disciples that without him, they can do nothing (see John 15:5). Without him, you cannot have a holy family as he had. Without him, family spirituality cannot exist.

Many Catholic parents have consecrated their families to Jesus. You may use your own words to give your whole family to Jesus, or you could use the following prayer.

Consecration of the Family to the Sacred Heart of Jesus and Immaculate Heart of Mary

Most holy Hearts of Jesus and Mary, united in perfect love, as you look upon us with mercy and caring, we consecrate our hearts, our lives, our family to you.

We know the beautiful example of your home in Nazareth was meant to be a model for each of our families.

We hope to have, with your help, the unity and strong, enduring love you gave to one another. May our home be filled with joy.

May sincere affection, patience, tolerance, and mutual respect be freely given to all.

May our prayers be filled with the needs of others, not just ourselves, and may we always be close to your sacraments.

Bless those who are present, as well as those who are absent, both the living and the dead; may peace be among us and when we are tested, grant us the Christian acceptance of God's will.

Keep our family close to your Hearts; may your special protection be with us always. Most Sacred Hearts of Jesus and Mary, hear our prayer. Amen.

The Sacraments and Family Spirituality

As Pope Paul VI writes, "The role of evangelization is precisely to educate people in the faith in such a way as to lead each Christian to live the sacraments as true sacraments of faith—and not to receive them passively or reluctantly."[10]

The Catholic Faith is communal. Communion with Jesus brings individuals to communion with each to make up the body of Christ. To bring your family to the sacraments is to participate in the greater Catholic community to encounter Jesus.

Here are some ideas to integrate the sacraments more fully into your family life:

1. Attend Mass as a family every Sunday and holy day of obligation.

2. Go to receive the sacrament of Reconciliation as a family.

3. As parents, help each of your children prepare for the sacraments of Reconciliation, Holy Eucharist, and Confirmation.

4. Attend Catholic weddings, baptisms, funerals, and ordinations of friends and extended family members with your children, both to celebrate with them and for their catechetical value.

Family Prayer

Years ago, Fr. (now Venerable) Patrick Peyton popularized the phrase, "The family that prays together stays together." Your family is a faith community because God dwells in each of its members. Family prayer is letting God live in your community of faith. Without prayer, your family's spiritual life would dry up like a branch not receiving the sap from the vine. Here are some simple ways to incorporate prayer in your family:

1. Teach your children to offer morning and night prayers.

2. Pray together before and after meals.

3. Pray for your family aloud when needs arise.

4. Pray before you leave for a car trip. Pray the Rosary on long rides.

---

[10] *Evangelii Nuntiandi*, 47

5. Pray novenas as a family. (Some examples: Christmas Novena, Divine Mercy Novena, Holy Spirit / Pentecost Novena).

Family Identity

Family identity is what makes families who they are, unique from other families. A family identity emerges as members of the family bond together through shared time, shared traditions, and shared values. It nurtures a sense of belonging and stability. Some families identify themselves as a musical family, a skiing family, or a camping family. Although these identities bring cohesiveness, they are based on what a family *does* together. To nurture a Catholic identity is to identify your family with Christ and his Church. This identity does not change, even when members of the family can no longer do specific activities together. Knowledge and faithful practice of the faith build family identity into a community of faith. Because missionary parents engage in ongoing faith formation, you can be the *first catechists* to your children and help them grow in their Catholic identity.

Here are a few simple ways to nurture a robust Catholic identity for your family:

1. *Celebrate baptism anniversaries* like birthdays.

2. *Have an altar in your home.* This is an exclusive place for a crucifix, a family Bible, rosaries, and statues. Sacramentals, holy pictures, and worship music lend themselves to learning the faith through the senses, especially for young children.

3. *Name your children after saints.* Children can learn more about their patron saint's life, and they can ask that saint to intercede for them.

4. *Celebrate Church feast days and liturgical seasons at home* to mirror what is being celebrated in your parish church. An awareness of the liturgical feasts and seasons allows your family to experience at home the Church's communal celebrations.

5. *Share your own faith experiences* with your children. This will allow your children to see how you have experienced God working in your life.

6. *Celebrate ethnic celebrations* and make these an opportunity to bring faith into the conversation. St. Patrick's Day is a good example. Even if

your family has no Irish ancestry, St. Patrick's life is truly an amazing "Catholic" story—and your family can ask for his intercession as well.

7. *Be alert for opportunities or teaching moments* to plant seeds of faith, hope, and love, such as the death of a loved one, the birth of a sibling, or a relative's wedding. These are powerful, teachable moments to present the Catholic understanding of these significant life events.

8. *Develop family rituals and traditions.* These repeated experiences for your family create family cohesiveness, reinforce family values, bring comfort, security, and lasting memories.

9. Choose a favorite family Scripture verse.

A Catholic home culture sustains a Catholic family identity. Your family culture is the collection of attitudes, ideas, ideals, and the overall environment of your family. The most significant way to nurture the Catholic Faith and live out a Catholic culture in your family is to express an attitude of openness to God and the teachings of his Church. The best thing about a Catholic culture is that it addresses the engagement of the whole person—mind, body, and spirit. The Catholic Faith offers all that is true, good, and beautiful. These transcendentals touch the innermost being of family members that make them truly human.

Family life, with all of its ups and downs, is a place of genuine joy.

Family Life

Every person is an essential member of the community because of the relationships they form with each other. Family life is more than just a shared space, shared time, and shared experiences. It also involves the interdependency of family members in living a communal life. Family life is a school for Christian development through obedience, charity, and mutual responsibility. It serves as a workshop for practicing virtues such as humility, justice, patience, and courage. As a microcosm of society, family life cultivates interpersonal skills and teamwork. A stable family life promotes a sense of belonging and connectedness and is a deterrent for strident individualism.

There are many factors that can hinder the development of a recognizable family life. The increased use of "screens" keeps family members separate, even when they share the same space. Sports and extracurricular activities demand time away from family life. Placing too high a priority to jobs and relationships outside the home can also contribute to a weak family life. The sad reality is that many families live as strangers because their daily lives do not intersect in a meaningful way. Without a true family life, relationships are shallow and the home becomes more like a hotel—a place where its members eat and sleep but have no recognizable communal life.

Here are some ideas to nurture a shared affection for the family:

1. *Assign chores.* Have each member of the family contribute to the work needed to keep the household running. This affirms the importance of the contribution of each member, and it will also help your children to develop a solid work ethic. Chores should correspond to each child's age, maturity, and ability.

2. *Work together.* Doing physical work together to get something done, such as washing the car, painting the fence, or raking leaves nurtures team-building towards a common goal.

3. *Have fun together.* Bonding through play and recreational activities strengthens the sense of camaraderie.

4. *Hold family meetings.* Communicating, sharing, getting input from family members on decisions to be made bring a sense of teamwork and respect.

5. *Reserve a family day.* This is a designated time for your family to be together. You could choose to watch a family movie, go out for ice cream, visit the grandparents, bake cookies, or to read an uplifting book (like the *Chronicles of Narnia*) together.

6. *Eat meals together.* This allows all members of the family to be together as a community.

7. *Support sibling relationships.* Since the relationship of siblings is often the longest relationship that individuals have in their lifetimes, fostering strong and loving relationships among your children means they will have them as trusted friends when they become adults. What a gift!

8. As an expression of support and an opportunity for family celebration, *attend together each family member's significant events.* One member's success is a success shared by the whole family, as is each challenge.

Hospitality

Hospitality as part of a family spirituality means opening up your family to others. It encourages members to learn the joy of giving. Welcoming guests and ministering to strangers, as well as serving the needs of others and evangelizing, are all efforts of hospitality. To be hospitable also means having an open heart towards others, consideration of others, being generous and doing acts for other's sake. Here are some ideas for your family:

1. Make meals for families with newborn babies or for bereaving families.

2. As a family, volunteer in a soup kitchen or other volunteer opportunities.

3. Invite new neighbors over for dinner.

4. Include others at family celebrations of Thanksgiving, Christmas, or Easter.

5. Attend parish gatherings to meet other families.

6. Bring Holy Communion as a family to shut-ins of your parish.

7. Befriend foreigners and immigrants in your community.

8. After discernment, be open to taking in foster children—or even adopting a child.

9. Engage in civic and political activities as a family, like joining a pro-life march together.

Integrated Love and Life

As you and your spouse continue to have a committed relationship with Jesus and the Church and an integrated personal and married spiritual life, you have sought to be missionary parents and intentionally lead your children into a vibrant family spirituality. The seed that died has grown roots, emerged as one trunk upright from the soil, and branched out to a crown of leaves and fruit. Your family tree has grown to be a beautiful living organism.

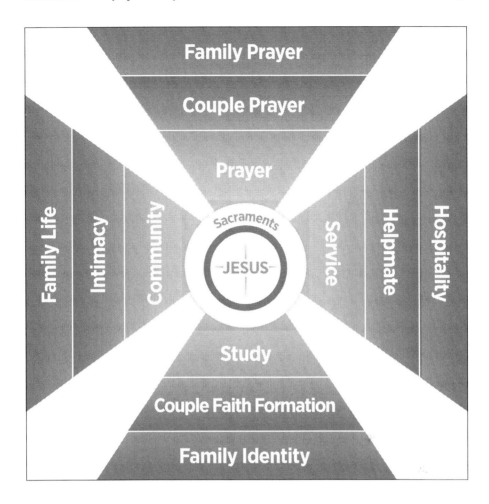

Integrated Love and Life

The image above shows the Catholic Discipleship Schema (the inner square), the Marital Spirituality Schema (middle square), and the Family Spirituality Schema (outermost square) together.

The Integrated Love and Life image shows how the life of discipleship grows to include significant relationships of spouses and children. The vocation of marriage and family indeed becomes the way of transformation and sanctification. For it is in relationships, in a communal life with others, that you mature in genuine love. Family life opens the possibility for the disciple to become increasingly selfless. As the disciple continues to mature in faith, grow deeper in identification with Christ, and grow in the fruit of the Holy

Spirit, your unity and love for your spouse and commitment to your family increases. Your family tree is truly alive because of the relationships among its diverse members and the indwelling of the Living God.

Keeping the Gates

God made us as social beings called to be in community with others. In marriage, God calls a man and a woman to a particular communion designed to bring forth children. A family is a unit of society. In fact, the family becomes the "interface" between the individual and society. Educator parents serve as *gatekeepers* for the flow of influence to and from their family units. As gatekeepers, you need to screen and regulate the effects of societal and cultural forces on your family. Today, parents often feel helpless in the face of the inundation of messages from social media, the educational system, and the current sociopolitical atmosphere, some of which express values that do not align with the values you seek to instill in your children. Ongoing faith formation for parents and maturation in your faith, along with the power of the Holy Spirit are ways to stand firm on Catholic teachings and strengthen your resolve to be effective gatekeepers. Your family can indeed be an influence on today's culture.

To build your family as a domestic church is to assert the Catholic Faith in society. With your Catholic formation, you, your spouse, your children go from your home to engage in activities, jobs, and movements in the public square, market place, and political arena. Your family members contribute to the betterment of society. Family members become carriers of God's love to others and agents for a civilization of life and love.

Keeping the Flow Free

Family life has a way of bringing out both the best and worst in you. Often, you choose to respond well to the demands of love for your spouse and children. You make sacrifices, give up your preferences, overcome your weaknesses in the name of service, and cling to the courage needed to ride through tough times. Other times, though, you allow the needs of self to win the day, and you insist on your ideas, methods, and goals no matter how they affect your spouse or family. Living in a community inevitably has challenges because it is a life of relationships. No one person is perfect in loving, so no relationship is perfect. Your faith community is no exception. Spouses offend each other. Children hurt each other. Members of the family disappoint each other. When the home is a school of Christian life, family members need to learn to ask for forgiveness and to forgive each other. Jesus renews hearts and renews relationships. He redeems persons and redeems families.

Receiving the sacrament of Reconciliation wipes away your sins and helps free you from those things that can become blocks in your relationship with God and your family. Sin blocks the sap in the vine and branches from flowing freely. In Reconciliation, an encounter with Jesus lifts you to begin anew in your resolve to love. This sacrament also gives you the grace to resist temptation. Going to confession is an opportunity the Church offers of which spouses, parents, and children should take advantage for the spiritual healing that leads to emotional and relational healing.

Before asking God to forgive your sins in confession, first forgive anyone who has done wrong to you. The Scriptures are definite that God will forgive you of your sins when you forgive those who have wronged you. Forgiveness of your spouse, children, family members, and others removes bitterness and resentment so you can again open your heart to loving others.

In preparing to receive the sacrament of Reconciliation, ask the Holy Spirit for help in examining your conscience and bringing to mind your sins. In admitting your sins as offenses against God and others, you recognize your failings. Sincere repentance is being sorry for your sins because they are offenses against the infinite love of God. In the person of the priest, you encounter Jesus, who died on the Cross for the forgiveness of sins and the salvation of souls. The priest gives you an act of penance to make retribution for the temporal effects of your sins and help you amend your life. A true exchange between you and Jesus occurs in this sacrament, through the ministry of the priest. After confessing your sins, the priest asks you to express repentance for them by praying an act of contrition. Sincerely asking Jesus to forgive you is at the heart of this part of the sacrament. This is based on the traditional form of the Act of Contrition:

> *"My God, I am sorry for my sins with all my heart. In choosing to do wrong and failing to do good, I have sinned against you whom I should love above all things. I firmly intend, with your help, to do penance, to sin no more, and to avoid whatever leads me to sin. Our Savior Jesus Christ suffered and died for us. In his name, my God, have mercy."*

The priest extends his hand over you and pronounces the words of absolution:

> *"God, the Father of mercies, through the death and resurrection of his Son has reconciled the world to himself and sent the Holy Spirit among us for the forgiveness of sins; through the ministry of the Church may God give you pardon and peace, and I absolve you from your sins in the name of the Father, and of the Son, and of the Holy Spirit."*

Then the priest dismisses you with, *"The Lord has freed you from your sins. Go in peace."*

This sacrament is a great gift. After experiencing the mercy, forgiveness, and healing of God in the sacrament, you are able in turn to be merciful and forgiving of your spouse, children, and others.

Keeping It Simple

Missionary parenting requires putting your marriage and family at a very high priority, which will require time and effort. It is wise to simplify. Simplicity is living your family life with only the essentials and removing those elements that do not align with your Catholic values. Here are four guidelines to consider to simplify your family life. These will guide both your small choices and big decisions in the years to come.

1. *Clearly convey.* As leaders of your family, have a clear and explicit plan for the overall growth and direction for your family. Write a family vision statement and communicate this vision regularly to family members to allow each member to be aware of family goals and direction.

   - Before the beginning of every school year, the Larson family holds a meeting to go over the reasons why they homeschool. This helps them remember why they embarked on homeschooling and directs the children towards clear family goals for the new school year.

2. *Intentionally move forward.* As your family grows and as your children develop and mature, update the plans that move everyone along in a logical flow to match their growing abilities. This gradual movement challenges them to go to the next stage.

- Every summer, Daren and Cecile make a simple plan for the coming school year with achievable goals for each of their children. Knowing the strengths and weaknesses of each child, they write down small action steps that each can work on during the year. They communicate this plan to each child.

3. *Properly align.* Make sure that all areas of your family life align with the values you are instilling to provide consistency and integration.

- When extracurricular activities require travel on the weekends, Frank and Jessica let the activity leaders know that their child needs to go to Mass either on Saturday evening or Sunday morning.

4. *Keep your focus.* Remain attentive and anchored to your family vision. Say no to activities or influences that are contrary to the values you want to instill and affirm Catholic values for your family.

- Aaron and Beth actively filter the movies and shows their children watch.

In forming family spirituality and communal life, missionary parents are as deliberate as the farmers who plan how they may achieve a bountiful crop yield at the end of the season.

Farmers decide what seed to buy, when to plant, how to fertilize, how to protect the plants from weeds and pests, and when to harvest. Many factors come into play of which farmers cannot predict or have control, like the weather. However, farmers remain diligent and hard-working to produce abundant crops. Missionary parents are intentional in including essential elements to form a spirituality for their faith community.

Deny Yourself, Pick up Your Cross, and Follow Jesus

Undoubtedly, raising a family takes a lot of work and demands attention and energy, especially when your children are very young. When missionary parents agree to give priority to raising their family, this explicit goal strengthens them and helps them move onward with determination. For most working parents, the home provides a refuge from the demands of work and a chance to rest and recuperate. It is a challenge to go home at the end of the day and encounter the needs of family life. The temptation is to attend to the immediate necessities such as meals, baths, and homework and put aside any family time or prayer. This is when you must seek grace to deny yourself, pick up your cross, and follow Jesus for the sake of your first community that exists to serve life and love.

Denying yourself means putting aside your desires in order to serve the needs of your family. In this case, being an active and loving leader of your community. This may mean working in such a way that all family members can contribute to the common good. It may include teaching children how to do their chores properly. Picking up your cross means persevering in implementing the plans you and your spouse designed for your communal life. To follow Jesus is to remain faithful to the mission that God gave you in your marriage. When you die to yourself, the seemingly daily and typical family interactions become bonds that secure your family as one community.

Gaining Ground

Before the settlers first plowed the soil in Iowa, the topsoil was fourteen to sixteen inches thick. By 2000, the average topsoil was only six to eight inches thick.[11] Plowing exposed the soil to erosion. If this erosion continues, Iowa's topsoil will continue to diminish. Erosion also describes the plight of families in the last few decades.

In the not too distant past, the vast majority of children were born into traditional nuclear families—that is, they were raised by married parents. In recent decades, however, the living arrangements of children have become increasingly varied and unstable—the institution of the family has been eroding. A vast number of children today are raised by divorced parents, who themselves are often the product of a divorced home.

The solution to both the erosion of topsoil in Iowa and of the family needs attention today. Scientists and farmers have the responsibility to address topsoil erosion, while disciples of Jesus in Christian marriages and families must reverse the deterioration of families beginning with their own. Healthy marriages lead to the stability of families. Holy marriages lead to the transformation of couples, children, and culture. Godly families raise fully-developed persons who can transform the world.

---

[11] Dettmann-Easler, 1999

TIME TO TALK

1. Does our family have a recognizable family spirituality? Do our children know we are raising them as Catholics?

2. Are we willing to be the leaders of this community? What can we do to foster a communal life in our family?

3. What are the present obstacles for a communal life?

PRAYER

Lord, make our family one, as the Holy Trinity is one. Our family belongs to you, Lord, and we also belong to each other. Help us to recognize each other's dignity and gifts. Help us to make a decision to intentionally build our family as one community. Send us Your Holy Spirit to make our first community be a home for faith, life, and love. We pray this in Jesus' name. Amen.

Chapter Five

FORM YOUR CHILDREN AS DISCIPLES OF JESUS

"Each child has a place in God's heart from all eternity; once he or she is conceived, the Creator's eternal dream comes true."

—Pope Francis

Seed-Bearing Fruit

Her father found Tingting seated by the dining room window one Saturday morning. The curtains were drawn open, and her face lifted to the sky. "What are you doing?" he asked her. "I want God to see me," she quietly replied. It was one of her first personal prayer times, wordless but full of desire, full of expectancy, full of a child's faith. At seven years of age, and the only child of her parents, Tinting had come to the United States from China so that her father could begin graduate studies at the university. When they arrived, they did not know God. While at the university, Tingting's father began attending a weekly Bible study group. Like most Chinese students, he was cautious about Christianity but was open to hearing about it. He shared with his family the new ideas he had heard, the Bible stories and the healing through answered prayer that he experienced. Tingting's father developed hepatitis as a result of receiving a tainted blood transfusion in China before he came to America. With the prayers and ministry of Christian friends, God miraculously healed him. From the sidelines, Tingting watched her parents' dread about the diagnosis, the proclamation of the Gospel and the care given by a Christian community, the hope that prayer instilled and the healing of her father's liver. These planted seeds of faith in her mind and heart that led her one morning to encounter God herself.

As Christian parents, we must consider the religious potential of our children—that is, their capacity for spiritual life. God, in his love, draws every person to himself. To disciple your children is to open for them a spiritual life that begins with a relationship with Christ— and missionary parents aspire to disciple their children.

To form your children as disciples of Jesus is to share the Christian life by living your discipleship with them. Jesus lived, ate, traveled, and taught his disciples in the three years of a shared life together. The dynamics of the communal life with his disciples were relational, intentional, and formational. To form your children as disciples is to help them develop as whole persons—integrated persons, who are in right relationship with God, others, and themselves.

One day, your children will leave home. As missionary parents, you hope that the seeds of faith, hope, and love that you planted by providing a Christian education will bear fruit in your children's lives.

Forming Your Children as Disciples and the Domestic Church

Forming your children as disciples of Jesus is helping your children to have a personal relationship with Jesus. This is the fifth key relationship in a domestic church. This actualizes the goal of Christian education. The domestic church is the first faith community and provides the relationships and environment that encourage children to become disciples. The most important relationship is with Jesus Christ, and parents support their children in living their baptismal dignity and promises. Catholic parents understand the nature of a person as a unity of body and soul. Their irreplaceable role of first educators and teachers of the faith to their children precisely is to provide opportunities for loving relationships with God, others, and the self. The domestic church is a community where parents and children grow in discipleship.

In looking at Christian education, Chapter Three highlighted the role of the educator, Chapter Four focused on the impact of the environment, and this chapter highlights the child in the education process.

Mysteries

The education that missionary parents provide has the most impact on children because it concerns the early years of growth and development. In this education, children are not so much students learning knowledge as they are persons learning to live as humans. The years from infancy to adolescence are foundational to the "forming" of the person. Catholic teachings on the value of a person and the social values mentioned in previous chapters are based on the Catholic understanding of the true nature of a person. In many ways, human nature is a mystery that Christians and their children enter into with faith.

The first Italian female pediatrician, Maria Montessori, spent many decades observing children, which helped her to map out the developmental stages of the child. She was one of the first scientists to observe children and discover their nature. From her work, she formulated the Montessori approach to education. Dr. Montessori was a Catholic who recognized and respected the religious nature of children. In her book *The Discovery of the Child,* she suggests that there are two "branches" of education that need collaboration: 1) the branch concerned with the nature of the child regarding external reality, and 2) the branch concerned with the nature of the child regarding supernatural life.[12] Christian education allows the two branches of education to come together as one process. The irreplaceable role of parents as first educators and teachers of the faith provides a complete education with the combination of the two branches of education. Even though each person has existed as a child, for the most part, childhood remains a mystery.

Fruit of Your Family Tree

When the time comes for a tree to produce fruit, buds sprout from branches, then they blossom and flower. Flowers are specialized structures that are involved in pollination and fertilization. After fertilization, a seed forms from a part of the flower. Another part of the flower develops to create fruit, which protects the seeds. A fruit develops skin and flesh and grows until it matures. Once mature, the fruit ripens. The process that the fruit undergoes from its initiation to the time it ripens comprises several stages. Each stage has particular characteristics and specific needs to move forward to the next stage. The process for the fruit is like the process for children to develop, grow, and mature. For both, the origin of the development and growth arises from within according to natural law. In general, these are stages of development and growth for the child:

- *Infancy – birth to age three.* This stage has the most considerable growth and transformation. The child has the need and capacity for relationship manifested in strong attraction to his mother's face and voice.

- *Early childhood – ages three to six.* The use of the senses is essential in learning about the environment. The child needs fixed points of reference around him. These lead to familiarity, security, and the internal order of his place in the environment.

---

[12] Gobi and Rojcewicz, 1998

- *Childhood – ages six to twelve.* This is a stable period of development when the ability for abstraction prepares them for formal studies. The stage also includes moral and social awakening and is a critical period for culture development. In the later part, a child needs models to help him with how to be responsible for his actions.

- *Early adolescence – ages twelve to fifteen.* The stage with significant changes in the body characterized by puberty.

- *Adolescence – ages fifteen to eighteen.* The child reaches sexual maturity, and the teen becomes an individual member of society.[13]

From infancy, your child becomes increasingly aware of himself and his environment. By the time he is eighteen, he can fully direct himself in that environment as well as in other circles beyond the family. The importance of self-direction or self-discipline cannot be overemphasized in your child's human development due to free will and the ability to make good or bad choices.

Obedience trains a child to gain control of his powers to direct them towards something objective. Learning obedience through the years in the family promotes the development of a will that is free to choose what is good, true, and beautiful.

The Child-Parent Relationship

The chapter on Missionary Parents highlights a Scripture verse that outlines the responsibilities of parents and children to each other. That chapter discussed the responsibility of parents to children. This chapter covers the first part of the verse that mentions the obligation of children to parents, "Children, obey your parents in the Lord, for this is right. Honor your father and mother." This is the first commandment with a promise, "that it may go well with you and that you may have a long life on earth" (Ephesians 6:4).

During their exodus from slavery in Egypt, God gave the Israelites the Ten Commandments. These laws served not only to form the Israelites as a people of God, but they also directed them on how to relate to God and others. The first three commandments pertain to giving God primary honor and allegiance, the fourth commandment is directed to children, "Honor your

---

[13]   Gobi and Rojcewicz, 1998

father and your mother, that you may have a long life in the land the Lord your God is giving you" (Exodus 20:12).

The fourth commandment spells out the duties of children to honor, respect, and obey their parents. It also applies to children who have matured, to honor and respect their parents in their old age or illness. Its place in the Ten Commandments demonstrates an order. The authority of parents flows from the authority of God. Jesus, who is the God-Son born as an infant to his Jewish mother and foster father, obeyed this commandment. As Scripture tells us, "He went down with them and came to Nazareth, and was obedient to them" (Luke 2:51). Jesus' obedience to God the Father was the basis of everything he said and did: "I did not speak on my own, but the Father who sent me commanded me what to say and speak" (John 12:49). As St. Paul states, "He humbled himself, becoming obedient to death, even death on a cross" (Philippians 2:8).

The parent-child relationship in the domestic church is a relationship designed by God. This design was not meant only for those who lived in Old Testament times; it is just as relevant today because it establishes a right order. Parents have great responsibilities towards their children, and children have the responsibility to respect the authority of their parents by obedience.

Obedience

Obedience means compliance with an order, request, or law, or to submit to another's authority. More than just the behavior of compliance, a training in obedience helps form the internal will of your child to obey. To listen, accept, direct the will, and act with the body describe the steps in obedience. Training in obedience orients the *I* of the child in the context of the relationship with parents. Obedience is gaining control of the self to direct the self towards someone else intentionally. Your child innately recognizes the authority of parents and must contend with it.

Teaching a child to obey and honor his parents depends on the parents. Given our fallen human nature, obedience, like any moral behavior, does not come naturally to a child but needs a formation of the mind and heart, and training of the will. Any relationship offers both privileges and responsibilities. Loving relationships come with "demands" or responsibilities that give form to that specific relationship. Obedience to you as parents prepares your child to have the ability to be in loving relationships with others, God, and the

Church. It develops the capacity to become a disciple. Obedience presents clear boundaries for the child, and when he acts within those boundaries, it paves the way for personal freedom.

Freedom and Boundaries

Setting clear boundaries brings security and promotes freedom to your child. Imagine living adjacent to a busy city street next to where your child goes out to play. Both the parent and the child perceive the danger. Having a fence brings freedom for the parents because they know that their child will be out of harm's way. Likewise, a fence brings freedom to the child in that he does not have to be mindful of how far to go into the yard to be safe. The fence brings a sense of security and a license to engage in play. Even if there is no perceived danger in real life, the uncertainty and lack of control over factors in life present parents and the child with the need to orient themselves. Boundaries and obedience are concepts that may not be emphasized because some think that they repress self-expression, creativity, or self-identity of the child. On the contrary, lack of boundaries and tolerance for disobedience promotes insecurity and lack of confidence.

Without expressed boundaries, a child is forced to orient himself in a vacuum with only the self as a reference point. This is not only a frightening proposition for a child, but it is unjust to have him face a situation beyond his capabilities to understand or to respond. Clear boundaries open up ample room for a child to have freedom of expression, directed creativity, and mastery of the self within the limits. Providing perimeters encourages the child's potentials to manifest because they express clear points of departure and arrival. Within these two points, the child experiences the liberty to act creatively. The experience of freedom within the established confines leads to confidence and independence. Master artists bound by the laws and limits of their medium are free to create their masterpieces. It is precisely the laws and restrictions of their medium that give form to the expression of their creativity.

Clear boundaries are an effective way to help your child strengthen his will by freely applying self-discipline to observe the limits. A child effectively learns freedom when accompanied by responsibility. It must also be made clear what happens when the boundaries are not maintained. You may reinforce your child's choice to uphold the boundaries with positive reinforcement while countering his decision to cross the boundaries with negative reinforcement.

- Our son, who was ten years old liked to play regularly with the boy next door. We determined how much time he could play depending on the schedule of that day, say an hour. He went with a watch, and he had to exercise his will to be mindful of the time and get himself home in one hour. When he came back on time, we usually said, "How was your time with your friend?" When he arrived late, we subtracted the number of minutes he was late from the next time he went out to play with the boy next door. Our son knew that within that hour, he was free to play and enjoy his friend's company, and he was responsible for meeting the expectation to be home on time. He had to wrestle with himself to peel off from playing when the appointed time came. This wrestling allowed him to flex his "will muscles" that strengthened his will as he chose to be home on time.

As each child grows in responsibility, parents give more freedom so that independence and self- discipline may grow. The child's growth in responsibility and freedom fosters self-confidence and builds trust between parents and the child. The funnel is an image for boundaries that parents may use to help their child in honoring and obeying them as the Lord commands.

- By the time our son was in high school, he frequently made plans to go out with friends on weekend evenings, and together we set the time he should come home. Almost always, he came home on the indicated time, or he called to say he would be late.

The Funnel

The funnel is a visual representation that can help parents understand the gradual increase of freedom and responsibilities that correspond to their child's growth and development. A funnel has a very narrow tube at one end and a cone that starts to gradually flare which ends with the broadest part at the other end. Imagine the funnel to be the eighteen years that you have to form your child's heart and mind. The narrow tube at one end represents the early years when the boundaries you set are very narrow to correspond to the child's ability to understand and take responsibility. This gives your child the time to gain control of his capacities and skills to actualize potential within those boundaries. Obedience is the successful control of the child over his mind and body to meet the expectations set before him. It is a practice to deny himself and act according to the directives of his parents. As your child continues to develop, when you observe that he is growing in personal responsibility, the boundaries widen. Freedom means allowing your child to express his personality, preferences, and methods within limits. As he matures, the boundaries may be negotiable to satisfy both child and parents, but accountability comes into play.

- When assigning chores, a specific outcome and a deadline give clear boundaries. The child is given latitude on how to meet those goals. For example: "These towels need to be washed, folded, and put away by tomorrow evening before our guests arrive at six o'clock." The teen figures out for himself when and how to meet these goals with his other responsibilities.

Parents keep their child accountable for the choices he makes. They do not overlook the instances when he chooses to cross the boundaries they have set. Depending on where your child is in the funnel progression, the consequences must be in proportion to the infraction and must be related to the wrong behavior (i.e., they must be "logical consequences").

- For example, hitting a sibling results in doing that sibling's chores for the day is an appropriate consequence, whereas not getting dessert has no connection to the sibling relationship.

When your child crosses the established boundaries, parents must determine if the infraction was done intentionally, which amounts to disobedience, or if it comes from a lack of ability due to your child's age or circumstances. This becomes a teaching moment to reinforce the required behavior.

As a child matures in his ability to make choices, parents allow for more freedom as he becomes increasingly responsible for his decisions. Responsibility means facing the consequences of the choices he makes. The only way your child will mature is if he has space and opportunities to use the tools he acquires. Self-determination will prepare him for more significant and complicated decisions that he will face as he engages in the world.

Inevitably, he will make mistakes. Picking himself up is a skill he has to learn while still at home, where the errors are not so costly. When parents allow the space and opportunities for making decisions, the child also has the chance to practice virtue in that the consistent choice of acting in goodness becomes a habit. Acquiring virtue requires action. It is not just an idea or attitude; it involves moving the will to express the "invisible" virtue through actions and behavior.

A person needs freedom to be virtuous. The freedom that disciples aspire for themselves and their children is the freedom experienced by the saints. Bishop Robert Barron offers an insight on the freedom experienced by saints as freedom for excellence where there is "disciplining of desire to achieve the good, first possible, then effortless."[14] The present-day view of freedom in our culture, the bishop continues, is the freedom of indifference, where the individual's inclinations and decisions dictate their choices. It is the first kind of freedom that evangelization offers because it is only in Jesus that this freedom is possible.

By the time your child turns eighteen, he may be out of the funnel. Hopefully, by this time, he has learned the function of boundaries which has to do with self-discipline. When your child leaves home, he should have the tools to set his internal boundaries. The funnel is a model that can help guide the transmission of the faith.

Transmission of the Faith Schema

The following Transmission of the Faith Schema is a diagram showing the essential components that are in place in children's lives when missionary parents establish and sustain a domestic church. This schema reflects what children reap when parents sow the essential elements of spiritual growth in their family.

---

[14] Bishop Robert Barron, homily "Being American, Being Catholic," July 4, 2010

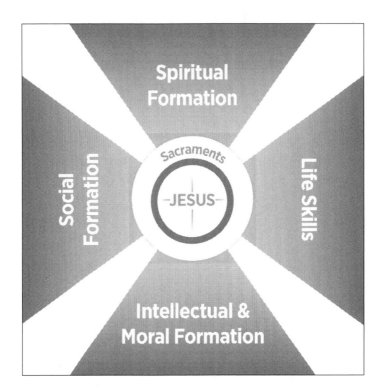

Transmission of the Faith Schema

- Your child knows Jesus and has a relationship with him.

- Your child knows and participates in the sacraments.

- Your child receives spiritual formation.

- Your child receives intellectual and moral formation.

- Your child receives formation regarding relationships with others.

- Your child acquires life skills.

These components of the transmission of the faith facilitate the full development of the child.

Relationship with Jesus

Teaching your children about God and witnessing a Christian life to them helps your children open their hearts to Jesus. Your attitude and openness to Jesus will influence, in no small degree, their attitude towards Jesus. As the *Catechism* says, "A wholesome family life can foster interior dispositions that are a genuine preparation for a living faith and remain a support for it throughout one's life" (CCC 2225). Missionary parents encourage their children to respond to the love of Jesus.

Missionary parents can depend on the pedagogy of the Church to teach your children about Jesus. The Church uses material things to point to spiritual realities that lend themselves for children to understand since they first learn through their senses. Parents can deliberately point Jesus out in all activities and things the Church says and does because everything she says and does points to him. Bringing attention to Jesus becomes a gentle proclamation of him to your children. Every Catholic church has a crucifix and a tabernacle, and the consecration of the bread and wine happens at every Mass. There are bells, incense, candles, and holy water that all point to Jesus. The liturgical feasts of Christmas, Easter, Ascension, and Pentecost mark the most significant parts of Jesus' life and mission on earth. The liturgical season of Advent tells of the prophecies about Jesus; the Christmas season presents the infancy narratives; Lent recounts Jesus' testing in the desert; the Triduum highlights the paschal narratives of Jesus; and the Easter season recounts and celebrates Christ's resurrection. If you read the Sunday Gospels weekly with your children and invite them to reflect on them, they will come to know Jesus. Of central significance is the real presence of Jesus in the Eucharist that parents help their children understand. In personally encountering Jesus in Holy Communion, children can grow in a loving relationship with him. Engaging your children in the Scriptures, the liturgy, and the sacraments touches not only their minds but also their hearts and helps them to understand and respond to the love of Christ.

The Sacraments and Forming Your Children as Disciples

The sacraments have the same efficacy on children as they do on adults. Jesus is as present to children as he is to adults. Teaching your children to prepare their hearts for the sacraments will help them receive all the intended grace from a particular sacrament. Help your children prepare and receive the sacraments of initiation (Baptism, Confirmation, and Holy Eucharist) and participate in worship with the Christian community to which you belong. The one-hour fast prepares you and your children to receive the Holy Eucharist at every Mass. What food does for the physical growth of your children, Holy Communion does for their spiritual growth. The sacrament of Reconciliation heals their souls from wounds of sin. Confirmation fills your children with the power of the Holy Spirit. The sacraments call them to live as children of God.

Importance of Identity

One of the essential truths that missionary parents can teach to your children is that through Baptism, they become *children of God*. From the perspective of eternity, the day of their Baptism is the most important day of their lives. Baptism frees them from original sin. They are incorporated in Jesus Christ, and they become adopted sons or daughters of God, acquiring full membership in God's family. Jesus was baptized to inaugurate his public ministry.

After his baptism in the Jordan River, Jesus' temptations in the desert by Satan were challenges to his identity as the Son of God: "If you are the Son of God ... " (see Matthew 4:3ff). Here, Satan presents three alternative identities to Jesus. He tempts Jesus to find his primary identity based on what he does (i.e., turn stones into bread), by what he owns (i.e., receive all the riches and kingdoms in the world if he worships Satan), and by the praise of others (i.e., put on a show by jumping from the tower without getting hurt). Jesus rejects all three temptations because he knew and accepted his identity as the Son of God. The earlier you can inspire your children to understand their identity as sons or daughters of God and teach them how to resist temptation, the more prepared they will be to live faithful lives as followers of Christ. As James 4:7 informs us, "Submit to God, resist the devil, and the devil will flee from you."

Parents make intentional decisions to teach and equip children not only to submit to God but also to resist the wily temptations of the devil, especially attacks on their identity as children of God. Listening to your children, especially discerning the underlying issues of what they are saying can reveal how they see themselves or how they want to be seen by others. These give clues on what identity they have embraced for themselves. A listening and understanding parent not only challenges these issues gently but reminds the child of their true identity because of their Baptism in Christ. Baptism is the beginning of a spiritual life that requires formation in order to mature.

Spiritual Formation

Spiritual formation refers to shaping the spiritual life, which is a lifelong growth towards union with God in Christ. Missionary parents help children begin this process. The home is a place where children experience and live the religious life through family life. Just as physical growth requires food, water, and air, spiritual growth requires spiritual elements. Love of God and others, intimacy with Jesus, avoidance of sin—both mortal and venial sins, growing in virtue, the forgiveness of others, and obedience all contribute to personal holiness. An intimate relationship with Jesus can be fostered by teaching your children about relational prayer.

Relational Prayer[15]

Teach your children relational prayer. This type of prayer is personal and helps them see that God cares for them:

- *Acknowledge.* Notice, name, and admit your thoughts, feelings, and desires. Be mindful of what is going on inside your mind and your heart.

- *Relate.* Choose to entrust what is in your heart to the Lord by telling him about it honestly. Share your thoughts, desires, feelings, and aspirations.

- *Receive.* Be receptive to God's response that may come as an insight, an image, an awareness of his presence, a peace, or even a correction. God may speak to you through events and people in your lives; be listening and attentive to the movements of the Holy Spirit.

- *Respond.* When you receive from God, respond accordingly. If you are called to act, then act. When you are invited to trust him, trust in his goodness and power. If you receive understanding and insight, let them guide you. When there is a correction, repent, and follow his way.

  ▷ When Steve and Lynn learned about relational prayer, they wanted to teach it to their children. For a year, they prayed

---

[15] Adapted from Fr. Scott Traynor, *The Parish as a School of Prayer: Foundations for the New Evangelization,* Institute for Priestly Formation, 2013

night prayers with them to model and coach them on how to pray in this way. After a year, their children prayed their night prayers using the relational prayer method. Steve and Lynn have commented on how beautiful it was to hear their children open up their hearts and share personal things about themselves in prayer.

Teaching Children Intimacy with God

Modeling intimacy with God in prayer is the best way to teach your children. If the habits and dynamics of intimate communication are part of your parent-child relationship, intimate prayer with God will feel normal and become a natural part of loving relationships.

- *Foster intimacy in family relationships.* Loved ones will learn healthy ways to express what is going on in their interior selves and also learn how to respond to others.

- *Pray with them.* When your children come to you and share their thoughts, feelings, and desires, respond by turning to God together, "Let us pray about this." Then, with your child, pray to God aloud, expressing to the Lord what your child has shared and together entrust it to him.

- *Encourage Relational Prayer.* As your older children share their innermost thoughts, feelings, and desires, encourage them also to share them with God, "When you pray today, tell God what is in your heart and be listening. I will also be praying about this for you."

As missionary parents, you should not underestimate the relationship between God and your children. When asked who is the greatest in the kingdom of God, Jesus responds in the following way: "He called a child over, placed it in their midst, and said, 'Amen, I say to you, unless you turn and become like children, you will not enter the kingdom of heaven. Whoever humbles himself like this child is the greatest in the kingdom of heaven. And whoever receives one child such as this in my name receives me'" (Matthew 18:2-5). The Bible also shows several instances when God spoke to children.

God Talks to Children

Some Bible stories where God reveals himself to children and they respond:

- A young boy, Samuel, hears God call his name in the night. Interestingly, God asks Samuel to deliver a personal message to Eli, the priest. This story is particularly striking in that God does not talk directly to the priest. Instead, he speaks to Samuel and asks him to deliver a message to the priest. Do you believe that God can speak directly to your child? Do you believe that God can use a child to deliver an important message to an adult? As parents, you can encourage a prayer life for your children that involves not only speaking to God but *listening* to him. God chooses Samuel to be a prophet. He "heard" his vocational calling early, and lived for many years as a prominent prophet. Samuel hears God tell him to go to Bethlehem to anoint the next King of Israel. There, Samuel goes to Jesse's house, and after looking at his older sons, he anoints the youngest son, David, who is a shepherd (see 1 Samuel 3, 16).

- The Scriptures report that when Samuel anoints David with oil, the Holy Spirit rushes upon David and remains with him. Indeed the Holy Spirit fills David's heart with the courage and grace to defeat the giant Goliath, and later to become the King of Israel (see 1 Samuel 16, 17). Through the story of David, the Scriptures again inform us that God cares for young children and that he has a plan or a calling for them. Our children receive the Holy Spirit at their Baptism.

- The angel Gabriel visits Mary when she is a young teenager. The angel does not say that Mary would be blessed after she gives birth to the Son of God; instead, the angel said that Mary, the young teen, is *already* "full of grace" (see Luke 1:26-38).

Finally, the apostles are complaining about parents bringing their children to Jesus. However, Jesus says, "Let the children come to me" (Matthew 19:14), He loves children, and he wants parents to bring their children to him.

Intellectual and Moral Formation

Intellectual and moral formation refers to shaping the use of reason—thinking, conceptualizing, and judging. Academic formation that includes the basic skills of reading, writing, and arithmetic that are learned in school must be further developed at home. These basic academic skills that parents help their children acquire are the foundation for their further intellectual and academic development. However, the intellectual and moral formation in the Transmission of the Faith Schema concerns developing a knowledge of the faith, which is essential to your children's growth as persons. These truths serve as guides and standards against which to judge one's actions. The Church has a wealth of intellectual and moral teachings that parents can hand on to their children. The transmission of the Faith includes catechesis, the formation of the conscience, and education on sexuality.

- *Catechesis* covers religious instruction in the fundamental beliefs of the Church, the liturgy and sacraments, moral formation, community life, missionary initiative, and prayer. The Church has a vibrant intellectual heritage that continues to speak truth to Catholics today. The Church teachings on faith and morals are dependable, and every disciple continues to gain knowledge and understanding.

  ▷ In observance of Advent or Lent, our family reads sections of the *YouCat* (a version of the *Catechism of the Catholic Church* for youth) after dinner.

- *Formation of Conscience.* As the *Catechism* states, "The education of the conscience is a lifelong task. From the earliest years, it awakens the child to the knowledge and practice of the interior law recognized by conscience ... [which] must be informed and moral judgment enlightened. Conscience is a judgment of reason whereby the human person recognizes the moral quality of a concrete act that he is going to perform, is in the process of performing, or has already completed" (CCC 1778). The *Catechism* goes on, "In the formation of conscience the Word of God is the light for our path, we must assimilate it in faith and prayer and put it into practice. We must also examine our conscience before the Lord's Cross" (CCC 1785). Including ethical principles when teaching moral behavior helps your children understand the *why* for an action.

  ▷ For example, telling your child to be quiet because the baby is sleeping will not be as effective as telling him that a baby has sleeping times and waking times and needs these times to grow properly—so we help the baby get his sleep. Telling the child to do or not do a specific behavior addresses only what is required for the present situation. Including moral principles, however, teaches the child to apply them to future cases of when the baby is sleeping.

Formation of conscience for children begins at infancy because the basis of the moral life is loving relationships. As they grow, the formation of conscience continues with a discipline based on rules. At about age six, the child has a moral awakening (the Church calls this the *age of reason,* when the child first receives the sacrament of Reconciliation). Children at this age naturally are open to laws and regulations because of their new consciousness of their responsibility in their behavior. The awareness of others in their lives moves them to want to know how to relate with or behave towards them. At this age, they need to learn what is right or wrong to help guide their wills. The Ten Commandments, clear communication of guidelines, rules in the classroom, the park, riding bikes, all speak to them. Learning board games or other games, in general, bring pleasure to children who discover their ability to understand and follow the rules. The rules help them to orient themselves in reference to others or the society and fosters responsibility for their actions. In older children, a need for heroes and models becomes important to learn how others respond to regulations and guidelines. The lives of the saints can help meet this need. During the teen years, adolescents will take ever more responsibility for their moral life. By the deepening of spiritual life and self-discipline, they can acquire virtue.

- The Church's teachings on sexuality are an integral part of the education for teens. Catholic teaching in this area has always given equal importance to the body, mind, and spirit. The virtue of chastity, precisely, is the integration of the body, mind, and spirit. Chastity is a virtue which parents encourage their children to acquire as they progress in their teen years.

  Teens are extremely interested in this area due to their sexual maturation. Providing them with a vision of healthy and joyful sexuality based on true love will help them make decisions about relationships.

  ▷ Many church youth groups include Theology of the Body teachings in their program. Various video series are available, both for teens and parents.

It is a great service to your children to help them learn and understand the Faith. Their formation in the Faith will engage their will to choose God for themselves. With grace, they can begin to live a Christian life from their childhood to adulthood. The formation of their hearts and minds impacts the many decisions they will face that determine the course of their lives.

Making Moral Choices

To equip maturing children in making moral choices, parents form their minds by teaching them the three aspects of an ethical choice. These three aspects are an action's 1) objective, 2) subjective, and 3) relative (situational) aspects. All three components are factors in making a moral choice.

- *Objective*: Does the action agree with God's law or not? If it does, then the decision is good and legitimate; if not, choose against this particular action.

- *Subjective*: Is this choice based on love or pride or self-gain? One discerns whether love or selfishness serves as the motivation for making a particular choice. Learning to evaluate personal motives for decisions takes training in thoughtfulness before acting. If motives are not pure, delaying making a choice is wise.

- *Relative (Situational)*: Is a choice appropriate for the current situation or circumstances? An excellent example to explain this aspect is the parable of the Good Samaritan (see Luke 10:25-37). A traveling priest and a Levite are heading to Jerusalem to pray. Prayer is objectively good, and probably the priest and Levite have proper self-motivation to pray. So, objectively and subjectively, they are making good choices to continue praying.

  However, when they see the man beaten by robbers, the situation demands that they change their plan and do the next loving thing, which is to care for the injured man. The choice to bypass the wounded man and continue to Jerusalem, is not a moral choice, because it fails on the relative part of the choice. As your children grow in understanding and their ability to reason, they can be taught all three aspects of making moral choices.

The exposure of children to different values, attitudes, and ideas in school, sports, and other groups will pose conflicting messages for those who have been raised in a domestic church. As Christian parents, you need to be diligent to equip your children to survive in the world around them with their faith intact. From grade-school onward, your child's capacity for intellectual understanding continues to grow, and he can, therefore, begin to understand the reasons for the Church's teachings. At home, present clearly and unapologetically the Catholic view of moral issues, particularly the controversial ones that your children face.

Because the Church has been endowed by Christ with his authority, we can trust the basic truth of her teachings on faith and morals. Children can be taught that there are logical reasons behind every teaching of the Church. In the end, the basic message to your children is that the Church's moral teachings uphold the dignity of persons and lead to an abundance of life.

Do not underestimate your children's ability to comprehend deep truths nor their openness to listen to what you say on important matters, even if they appear to be uninterested. For your children to reject these reasons as they grow older, they will need to have reasons for why they disagree.

Today, the battle between truth and lies rages in your and your children's minds. What we believe manifests in our decisions, ways of life, and worldview. Truth, as revealed by Jesus and safeguarded by the Church, must be the "lighted lamp that is not put under a bushel basket; but set on a lampstand, where it gives light to all in the house" (Matthew 5:15). If you have engaged in your lifelong faith formation, you should be well equipped to form your children's minds with the truth. The missionary parents' job is to announce and proclaim with words and actions.

Social Formation

Social formation is the process of learning to interact with others. Very young children spontaneously absorb the culture of their family as they observe and imitate its members. They learn the "norm" of behavior in the family and adopt it so that they are in harmony with the family environment. Living out Catholic social values in the communal life of the family helps teach these values to your children. Social skills such as communication (i.e., active listening and verbal and non-verbal ways of communicating), teamwork, negotiation, and conflict resolution are learned. Every family has patterns of interaction, and the parents' interpersonal skills have established many of the patterns. Some are healthy patterns, while others may be unhealthy. To help children acquire effective interpersonal skills, parents must assess their own skills and must come together to decide what culture they wish to provide their children. Many Christian authors offer parenting wisdom that you can find and are worth your efforts to learn. Here are a few things to consider:

- *Respect.* Besides respect for parents, children also learn respect for authority, the elderly, their peers, the property of others, and nature. Basic grace and courtesies like *please, thank you, and May I* are simple to teach and acquire. The Golden Rule, "Do unto others as you would have them do unto you," speaks even to young children.

- *Asking for forgiveness.* To recognize that one has hurt another takes humility. Asking for forgiveness and forgiving others when they hurt you are part of a healthy family culture. Modeling forgiveness helps children to see how it is done and will give them the language to use. When family members recognize their faults and weaknesses, they can have a sense of solidarity with others when they fail, and this helps them to be merciful to those who have wronged them.

- *Healthy expression.* Parents and children get frustrated, disappointed, angry, and irritated, which can make day-to-day interactions difficult. Parents can teach their children healthy ways to express negative emotions so that they become more effective in dealing with these emotions themselves which helps them to understand others experiencing negative emotions.

- *Little things matter.* Not interrupting someone in conversation, turning off the lights when not in use, or even replacing an empty toilet paper roll with a new one and a million small things in family life can show care and consideration for other members of the family.

Life Skills

The practical life skills necessary for children to learn are developed by serving. Every family member contributes to the family's communal life. In childhood, the care of self and care of the home are beginnings of learning practical life skills. These practical skills will help children in their future lives to serve others. Service also builds a work ethic beginning at an early age. Time management and money management are skills that they need to acquire in their teen years when they manage their schedules and earn money from jobs.

- In our family, three conditions are non-negotiable and not open to discussion: 1) matters of safety, 2) matters of right and wrong, and 3) chores. When our children have requests or express desires, these three non-negotiable conditions are reviewed to come up with the appropriate response. The issue in question must be safe, ethical, and not interfere with the completion of chores.

Step-by-Step, Year-by-Year

Before school begins in the fall, we make a plan for each of our children for the coming year. Since they are a year older, a bit more mature, and more capable of doing a variety of work, we set some goals that serve as guides for us as parents.

We go over four areas in which each of our children can grow during the year: spiritual formation, moral character formation, intellectual formation, and practical skills. When our children were young, we had a few simple goals, such as learning how to pray the Our Father, to say *May I* and *thank you*, to read, and to set the dining table. At the beginning of each new academic year, we reviewed each child's progress on their goals from the previous year. Taking into account each child's personality, age, strengths, and weaknesses, we selected the goals for the coming year. As our children became older, the goals were clearly shared with them, and they began to assume personal responsibility. Each of our children has a notebook containing all their annual goals since kindergarten, i.e., five years old. They like leafing through to see the goals they achieved in past years. As parents, our job in this was not so much daily reminding them of these goals, but it was to provide plenty of opportunities for these goals to be reached. We provided the home, the community, the encouragement, and the affirmation.

- As a family we prayed before bedtime and incorporated the Our Father. At Mass, we cued the child when the Our Father was about to be prayed.

The setting of small but clear goals in these four areas act like guides for actions and choices for parents and children. This plan instills core values gradually and begins virtue through the practice of their will. It also prepares children to listen to God's call for their lives.

Preparation for Vocation

Catholic disciples know that Jesus calls each person to a specific vocation, which is both the path for sanctification for him or her and a call to serve the kingdom of God, the path for greatest love. As Catholic parents, you have the mission to help your children discover or hear their vocational call. Introduce to your children the different vocations (i.e., marriage, priesthood, consecrated religious life, blessed single life) by letting them know that you are praying for them to discern their vocation and by encouraging them often to be listening to God.

God has a particular plan for your children that will give meaning and purpose and bring them joy. The path ahead for them may not be so clear or defined, but it is a call to love. The domestic church prepares your children to hear the call of Jesus for them and equips them to respond to this call. With the Transmission of Faith Schema in place, your children acquire habits that prepare them for discipleship.

With prayer, the sacraments, the Scriptures, and faith formation, your children become familiar with the voice of God. Through engagement with community and service, your children will grow to be aware of their gifts and use them to meet the needs of others. With the formation of conscience, they will have an internal order that will guide decisions. Regardless of the vocation of each child, all require hearing God's call, responding to that call, living in community, serving others, and the need for grace from the sacraments to faithfully live the vocation. The domestic church prepares your children to respond to God when they discern their vocation.

Deny Yourself, Pick up Your Cross, and Follow Jesus

The handing down of the faith calls parents to teach the faith to their children because their children are the next generation of Catholics. When totalitarian regimes suppress the practice of Christianity, the prohibition of the passing of the faith to the next generation leads to the "godlessness" of succeeding generations. (This has been shown in former communist countries, which promoted atheism and persecuted believers for decades.) The inaction by just one generation to hand down the faith erodes the Christian faith in family life and the culture.

It is easy for parents to brush aside your irreplaceable roles as first educators of the faith to your children because systems are in place that also handle this duty. Teachers, coaches, child-caregivers, mentors, and other services are readily available. Many parents have the idea that they are not competent enough to be the educators or teachers of the faith to their children. Yet these same parents display extraordinary diligence in study and intentional practice of specific actions when, for example, their child has a peanut allergy. Eco-conscious parents explicitly educate their children on how to recycle, conserve energy, and reduce their carbon footprints. Every day, parents commit their time and treasure to sports activities and all sorts of extra-curricular engagements for their children. The question is not ill-preparedness but priority. If you value the inherent dignity of your family members, believe in the preeminent effect of grace, and are willing to sacrifice so that your family members can taste real freedom and joy, you can build a domestic church. This is where you must die to yourself, pick up your cross, and follow Jesus—for the sake of your children, the Church, and the future of the world.

One of St. Teresa of Calcutta's famous quotes applies to Catholic parents, "God does not require that we be successful, only that we are faithful." Be faithful to God in the mission of Christian parenthood in which he has called you, and leave the results in his hands. He calls parents to transmit the faith to their children.

As the Lord instructs the people of Israel, "Take to heart these words which I command you today. Keep repeating them to your children. Recite them when you are at home and when you are away, when you lie down and when you get up. Bind them on your arm as a sign and let them be as a pendant on your forehead. Write them on the doorposts of your houses and on your gates" (Deuteronomy 6:6-9). These words, of course, also apply to us as Christian parents who seek to build a domestic church.

What is God referring to in the preceding verses? He is referring to the verses just before these, when he proclaims, "Hear, O Israel! The Lord is our God, the Lord alone! Therefore, you shall love the Lord, your God, with your whole heart, and with your whole being, and with your whole strength" (Deuteronomy 6:4-5). Parents are to faithfully repeat the Great Commandments to their children so that they may incorporate them into their minds and hearts and integrate it into their lives. Christian parents proclaim Jesus Christ, who suffered, died on the cross, rose from the dead, ascended into heaven and will come again. This is the Good News that your children will first hear at home—the foundational message of their lives.

When the Fruit Falls from the Tree

Although your domestic church is your children's first faith community, it is not the last. Your children's initiation to the Christian life does not solely rest on you as parents. It is crucial to introduce them to a broader Christian community. "The parish is the Eucharistic community and the heart of the liturgical life of Christian families" (CCC 2226). It is the whole community that proclaims Christ, and children must enter into contact with this community. Children will witness members of the community confirm the Christian teachings in the way they live their lives.

Missionary parents know that each child, because of his dignity and free-will, has to choose for himself to follow Jesus as he emerges into adulthood. Ultimately, knowing that each of your children belongs to God, you entrust them to his mercy for the rest of their lives. Your children must choose to open their hearts to the call of Jesus. Only they can choose to be the seed that dies.

Inside a seed is an embryo of the plant, with its potential roots, trunk, branches, and leaves. The fruit which holds the seed is the way it separates from the tree and is carried somewhere else to produce another tree. When your children are "out of the funnel" and on their own, the hope is that, as they fall like fruits from the family tree, they will choose to be the seed that dies and become disciples of Jesus. They can grow rooted close to the living water.

TIME TO TALK

1. Take the time to pray for each of your children, thanking God for each of them and asking God for the grace for each one of them to grow in faith, hope and love.

2. Do we have a priority of handing down the Catholic Faith to our children?

3. What are the most important things we can do for or teach our children?

PRAYER

Giver of all life, thank you for the gift of each of our children. You have a plan for each of them and you love them more than we could ever love them. They belong to you, Lord, and we entrust them to you. Help us to guide them with our words and deeds. Open their hearts to know, love, and serve you. In Jesus' name we pray, Amen.

Chapter Six

INTEGRATE INTO THE CATHOLIC CHURCH

"The Church is a family of families, constantly enriched by the lives of all those domestic churches."

—Pope Francis

God with Us.

The Chinese priest, pastor of a small parish in a northwest China village, unlocked a small windowless room on the second floor, and we all took off our shoes as our family followed him into the room with the floor covered by a handmade mat. The room was empty except for a low table at one end of the room. On the table was a small box, and on each side of the box was a flickering electric candle. The priest, who wore street clothes, knelt and bowed very low with his forehead almost touching the mat. We made the same gesture. On closer look, the table was an ordinary coffee table, and the small box was a cheap jewelry box like a small armoire with a clock on it that did not have the correct time. The clock was not running. Our children whispered, "Where is the tabernacle?" The priest pointed to the jewelry box as if he understood what our children asked. The children tried to restrain their giggles. Their gleeful amusement at an unexpected tabernacle with a clock was muted by a great effort to be reverent in the presence of Jesus. Despite the unique style of the tabernacle, the children acknowledged the real presence of Jesus in the Eucharist reserved inside.

We all knelt silently in the makeshift Blessed Sacrament reservation chapel, yet in our hearts, we praised God, "Glory to God in the highest!" Jesus has come to this place that would qualify as one of the "ends of the earth." As Scripture proclaims, "The people in darkness have seen a great light; on those living in the land of the shadow of death, a light has dawned" (Matthew 4:16). The ten Catholics in that ancient village persuaded the local bishop to send a priest to establish a parish. Since the priest's arrival, in a short period of time, many locals were baptized, and the growing church gathered for Mass in a room on the third floor of the small building. We joined them on several Sundays, and even without comprehending a word of the spoken Chinese language, we felt at home in the parish.

Jesus promises his disciples, "And behold, I am with you always, until the end of the age" (Matthew 28:20). By the power of the Holy Spirit, Catholics continue to enjoy the real presence of Jesus in our midst today.

Integrating the Domestic Church into the Catholic Church

Integrating your family into the Catholic Church is the sixth and final key relationship essential to a domestic church. Jesus established the Church to be his continual presence in the world—Emmanuel, God with us. When a family is integrated into the Catholic Church, family members live in the presence of God. The Church has a term for this—*communion*. The baptized are in communion with the Blessed Trinity and with each other in a love that never ends. Part of the irreplaceable role of Catholic parents is to bridge their first faith community to the universal faith community, which is the Church.

If Christian marriage stands as one bookend of the domestic church, the Church stands as the other bookend of the domestic church. A domestic church cannot fully function or survive as a domestic church unless it is integrated into the Church because of its need for grace. Grace is God's gift of his divine life. Grace is not a commodity to be acquired but life in relationship with God, given by God and lived by us.

The Church has its origin in the will of Jesus when he says, "You are Peter, and upon this rock, I will build my Church" (Matthew 16:18). In the Incarnation, the Word became flesh, and today, the Incarnation is present in the body of Jesus, the Church. Jesus is present in our midst—in the Scriptures, the community of the baptized, the person of the priest, and the sacraments, most especially in the Holy Eucharist.

Catholic disciples, in their intentional relationship with Jesus, receive a renewed love and commitment to the Church. When they marry and have children, they look to the Church for the grace necessary to sustain their domestic church as well as the grace needed to contribute to the life of the Church.

- Jesus was born into a first faith community—his family in Nazareth. Jesus was raised as a faithful Jew by his parents' teaching, observance, and practice of their Jewish faith. Their participation in the Jewish community, obedience to its laws, living out their identity in Israel as the Chosen People was part of the Messiah's developmental years. Jesus was circumcised, presented in the Temple, and made pilgrimages to the Temple according to Jewish law and customs. Mary and Joseph integrated their faith community into the greater Jewish community and tradition. Jesus died as a Jew. However, he is the Messiah, the Savior of the world. The blood he shed on the Cross transformed the Old Covenant into the New and established the Church.

As Pope Francis says, "Reflecting on the interplay between the family and the Church will prove a precious gift for the Church in our time. The Church is good for the family, and the family is good for the Church."[16]

Mutual Dependence

The relationship of the family to the Catholic Church is like that of a single cell to the human body, the relation of a basic unit to the whole. A cell removed from the body will not survive on its own. Every cell is vital because their unity forms the whole organism that has life, and reciprocally, the body sustains life for all the cells in it. Every domestic church is a unit of the body of Christ that cannot survive on its own, but its proper function contributes to the life of the Church. The Church, in turn, functions to give divine life to all the domestic churches that comprise it. Jesus clearly illustrates this relationship in the parable of the vine: "I am the vine, you are the branches. Whoever remains in me and I in him will bear much fruit, because without me you can do nothing. Anyone who does not remain in me will be thrown out like a branch and wither; people will gather them and throw them into a fire, and they will be burned" (John 15:5-6). Without the divine life of grace, there is no life nor fruit for the domestic church.

- Scott and Dianne explain that they began their marriage with no faith or a faith community. In the first six years of their marriage, they had three children, and the demands of raising small children challenged their relationship. They considered divorce. Their parents were divorced, however, and they did not want their children to grow up in a broken home like they experienced. As they looked for a better option, some friends introduced them to NFP.

  They then came to understand, for the first time, God's intent and design for marriage and family. Their journey led them to the Catholic Church. Today, they are committed Catholics, and they hope to have more children. They openly share that they now experience a fullness of life in their marriage relationship and in their family that

---

[16] Pope Francis, *Amoris Laetitia,* 86-88

they attribute to their faith in God and participation in the Catholic Church. Scott and Dianne discerned that God was calling them to be NFP teachers to give to others the gift that they had received.

The Church is the body of Christ, and it has many parts. Each part is needed for the life of the whole body. Building a domestic church where there is faith, hope, and love is an excellent service in strengthening the entire Church.

Grand Scheme

The schemas presented in this book are patterned after the Church's grand scheme of a people growing to love God and love others. The schemas in previous chapters are diagrams that show the essential components of growing in love of God and others that are made specific to the different relationships in the domestic church. In the Church, the grand scheme holds Jesus as its center.

- Jesus is the cornerstone of the Church, her beginning and end, the author and perfector of her faith.

- The Church's life is closely bound to the sacraments through which Jesus encounters his followers in real time.

- Worship, liturgy, and prayer are activities that the Church has engaged in for two millennia, as she recognizes the spiritual nature of the relationship between God and his family. Thousands of Catholic churches can be found in many parts of the world that give testimony to generations of people who have gathered to worship and pray to God.

- The Church offers a rich intellectual and moral heritage that is as relevant today as it has been for centuries. Her work supports the ability of persons to seek truth and grow in understanding. In addition to the collected spiritual writings and inspired works of holy men and women, the Church developed universities as institutions for study and intellectual growth.

- The Church is involved in the local affairs of communities by ministering to the physical and material needs of people, particularly for the poor, the sick, the orphans, and widows. The Church provides a face for our merciful God in caring for the homeless, disenfranchised, immigrants, and many others in dire situations. This mercy can be seen particularly in her care for the sick, and hospitals built by the Church provide care for them. About thirty-five percent of hospitals in the United States are Catholic hospitals.

- Outreach in service and evangelization are primary mission activities of the Church.

  Social justice teachings and work to inform and help guide government and political-economic structures to improve life for the disadvantaged continue to be emphasized today. Evangelization has received renewed efforts in the Church today.

These activities of the Church are the fruit of love that the presence of Jesus in the Church and the power of the Holy Spirit continue to produce in his body united to him. The domestic church, as a unit of that body, also produces these fruit of love within the existing relationships when it is integrated into the Church.

Marks of the Church

The Church is the enduring visible yet spiritual, human yet divine presence of God in the world, just as Jesus is both God and man. Because of this mysterious nature of the Church, she can minister to human beings who are made of body and soul. The four marks of the Church display the Church's structured yet Spirit-led characteristics. These marks are attributes of the Church that form a summary of the most important affirmations of the Christian faith: "We believe in one, holy, catholic, and apostolic church." We proclaim these words in the Nicene Creed every Sunday at Mass. As basic units in the body of Christ, the domestic church is imbued with these same marks because of the presence of Jesus and the power of the Holy Spirit.

The Church is One

The Catholic Church is the one church founded by Jesus Christ. It is anointed by the one Holy Spirit who unites all baptized members to God and each other in one faith and worship. The domestic church, along with the universal Church, adheres to the one set of doctrine that the Church teaches which is revealed by God in the Scriptures and Sacred Tradition. The Church is

Christ's body, of which he is the Head. Moreover, Catholics are in communion with one another as well as with the Blessed Trinity.

- As a soil scientist, I (Bob) travel to many places and countries in the world to collaborate with other scientists. I can appreciate the *oneness* of the Church in being able to go to Mass on Sundays and know that the worship, the Scripture readings, the sacrifice being offered are the same as what my family is experiencing back home. In Holy Communion, my family and I are in communion with each other despite the physical distance separating us. We are spiritually in union with each other, with the Body of Christ, and with the Blessed Trinity.

The Church is Holy

The Church is holy because she has been washed in the blood of the Lamb. Jesus' sacrifice on the cross takes away sin and restores the Church to her original holiness. As the Bride of Christ, Jesus sanctifies the Church with his passion, death, and resurrection and continues to purify her. The domestic church is holy because each baptized member is a dwelling of the Blessed Trinity. The integration of the family into the Church makes them the "living stones" that build the edifice where God dwells. The Church is made holy through the presence of Christ, and he channels his holiness through the sacraments. Parents and their children go to the sacraments to encounter Jesus and receive grace to live holy lives.

- A few years ago, our diocese compiled a list of the "Top Ten Reasons to Be Catholic." Diocesan leaders asked individuals, groups, organizations, families, and parishes to submit their ten reasons why they are part of the Catholic Church. The number one reason is the Eucharist. The essential gist of the submitted responses was "Jesus is our number one reason for being Catholic. We believe the Eucharist *is* Jesus. Jesus' sacrifice, his self-gift on the Cross, continues to be made present in the celebration of the Mass, where through the Eucharist we receive Jesus himself and are brought into union with God and communion with one another."

The Church is Catholic

The word *catholic* comes from a Greek word meaning "universal"—and the Church certainly is universal, spread throughout the world, with a message intended for every people and nation. The domestic church is a part of a parish, which in turn is part of a diocese, which is part of the universal Church. The pope is the visible head and universal pastor of the Church. The Church is more than its visible aspects; it is the mystical body of Christ, a family. This mystical family includes all the baptized in all the places on earth and all the faithful who lived in the past and are now in heaven or purgatory.

- Nearly every summer, Will and Millie take their children on a long road trip to a national forest or to visit relatives in different parts of the country. Whether on the road or at their destination, they find a Catholic Church to attend Sunday Mass. They have attended Mass in cathedrals in cities, in small churches in rural communities, and Newman centers close to colleges.

The Church is Apostolic

Jesus established the Church upon the apostles, with Peter as its head (see Matthew 16:18), to spread the Gospel and hand on his teachings. The teachings of Christ are handed down by the teaching authority of the Church given it by Jesus himself, and the Gospel message is transmitted through the generations through *apostolic succession*. The Church holds the "deposit of faith"—all the truths Jesus entrusted to her—from the apostles, and their successors, the bishops, faithfully hand this on to us today. The mission of the Church is to evangelize, and *apostle* means one who is "sent." The Church continues to send the baptized to go out to proclaim the Gospel in their words and actions.

- Living in a university town, the Browns invite international students to their family holiday celebrations. Many of the international students come from different religious traditions. The Browns always share with their guests the significance of the holidays they are celebrating, such as Christmas, Easter, and Thanksgiving. Their family offers hospitality as well as the Good News.

When Catholic parents establish their domestic church, which draws its life from the larger Church, the four marks of the Church—one, holy, catholic and apostolic—are evident in their family. For more than two millennia, persecutions, heresies, schisms, scandals, and conflict have afflicted the Church, but "the gates of hell shall not prevail against it" (Matthew 16:18). As Pope Leo XII writes of this verse, "The meaning of this divine utterance is, that, notwithstanding the wiles and intrigues which they bring to bear against the Church, it can never be that the church committed to the care of Peter shall succumb or in any wise fail."[17]

The preceding words imply that there is an ongoing battle between forces of evil and the Church. The domestic church can also feel this struggle and needs to engage in it. The hope for the domestic church rests on the confidence that the Church has in God—the Father, Son, and the Holy Spirit—as her provider, protector, and preserver. The domestic church exists not solely as a family but as a community with a spiritual life animated by the Holy Spirit, who protects and preserves it. The Church continues to thrive because she is not merely a human organization but a divine institution, animated by the Holy Spirit.

The marks of the Church have their source in Jesus, and the Eucharist is the sacrament in which his presence becomes visible—and through which the Holy Spirit deepens these marks. The Eucharist is the "source and summit" of our Faith because the whole life of the Church is ordered by it, and everything in the Church is ordered toward it.

The Eucharist – Source and Summit

The Eucharist is the true Presence of Jesus in its fullness—body, blood, soul, and divinity—the fullness of grace itself. Participating in Mass, your family experiences the presence of God in word and sacrament. In the Liturgy of the Word, Catholics assume the open position of "Hear O, Israel!" as the proclamation allows God to reveal himself to every person in every generation. Jesus speaks words of everlasting life to those with ears of faith. In the Liturgy of the Eucharist, the sacrifice of Jesus on the Cross is made present. At Mass, we are living the New Covenant in a concrete way.

In the preparation of the gifts at the beginning of the Liturgy of the Eucharist, the priest makes a gesture called *epiclesis,* when he extends his anointed hands over the bread and wine to invoke God the Father to send the Holy Spirit on the gifts being offered. He is asking that the Holy Spirit change the bread into

---

[17] Pope Leo XIII, *Satis Cognitum* ("The Unity of the Church"), 12

the "bread of life" and the wine into "our spiritual drink." The priest says the words of consecration, the words of Jesus, to institute the Holy Eucharist,

"Take this, all of you, and eat of it, for this is My body, which will be given up for you."

"Take this, all of you, and drink from it, for this is the chalice of My Blood, the Blood of the new and eternal covenant, which will be poured out for you and for many for the forgiveness of sins."

This is the most solemn and miraculous part of the Mass because this is when God acts to transform bread and wine into the real presence of Jesus. The priest first elevates the host, then the chalice. In these sacred acts, the Holy Spirit makes present the once-for-all sacrifice of Jesus on Calvary to God's people in the current time.

The priest continues in the Eucharistic Prayer and asks Jesus, through the Holy Spirit, to unite all those present to the Church spread throughout the world, to all people of the world, to those who have died, and to Mary and all the angels and saints in heaven. Jesus, in the consecrated host, unites all peoples and all things to himself and offers them up to the Father in the one sacrifice of praise. At the elevation, the priest raises the paten and chalice, offering the perfect sacrificial Victim to the Father in the Holy Spirit with all the faithful united in the sacrificial offering:

"Through him, and with him, and in him, O God, almighty Father, in the unity of the Holy Spirit, all glory and honor are yours, forever and ever."

Amen.

Collectively, we then pray "Our Father, who art in heaven…" With one voice and one heart addressing God the Father, everyone in attendance stands side by side as children of God.

The reception of the Holy Eucharist renews the children of God, as the passion, death, and resurrection of Jesus Christ bears fruit in our lives. This is where plentiful redemption that Jesus won for us comes to each believer in a particularly tangible way. As the priest or Eucharistic minister proclaims to each communicant, *"The Body of Christ,* " and *"The Blood of Christ,"* we respond, *"Amen,"* (Yes, I believe) and receive them. We receive the Lamb of God, who takes away the sins of the world. We receive our Savior and salvation. With each reception of the Holy Eucharist, Catholics receive, "in Christ every spiritual blessing in the heavens" (Ephesians 1:3). Receiving Holy Communion is a true encounter with the Risen Lord, where Jesus and the communicant are united to each other and Jesus unites each one to his body, the Church.

Effects of Holy Communion

It comes to bear that the Eucharist is the source and summit of the domestic church. Consider these fruits of Holy Communion on your soul and the souls of your family members (see CCC 1391–1397):

- The principal fruit of receiving the Eucharist in Holy Communion is an intimate union with Christ Jesus.

- Holy Communion preserves, increases, and renews the life of grace received at Baptism.

- Holy Communion, at the same time, cleanses us from past sins and protects us from future sins.

- The Eucharist strengthens our charity, and this living charity wipes away venial sins.

- The Eucharist preserves us from future mortal sins.

- Through the Eucharist, Christ unites the faithful in one body— the Church.

- The Eucharist commits us to the poor.

Hearts that receive Jesus become living tabernacles. In the Eucharist, lies the power of discipleship, marital spirituality, missionary parents, family spirituality, and the domestic church. The Holy Eucharist is medicine for their illnesses. In this sacrament of unity, disciples and families are bound together by the passion, death, and resurrection of Jesus Christ. In Holy Communion, the presence of Jesus has been made continual over two millennia to the present day. The presence of God resides in his family, the Church.

The Family of God

Integrating your family into the Church means participating and contributing to the family of God. Missionary parents must understand that your integration into the Church contributes significantly to the presence of Jesus in the Church. Your family is an essential part of the Church, especially in its worship and communal prayers. As St. John Chrysostom writes, "You cannot pray at home as at church, where there is a great multitude, where exclamations are cried out to God as from one great heart, and where there is something more: the union of minds, the accord of souls, the bond of charity, the prayers of the priests" (CCC 2179).

Because your domestic church is part of the family of God, you, your spouse, and your children have a significant responsibility towards the Church. Catholics experience solidarity in journeying in faith together - helping one another and being strengthened by others.

- At their parish, the Forker family signed up to bring Holy Communion to the residents of a nursing home in town. On the first Sunday of every month, they visit the residents to tell them about the Sunday readings, pray with them, give them the Eucharist, and sing a hymn with them.

The parish is the most immediate faith community where your family has an impact on its life and care. There are many needs and ministries in every parish that depend on the involvement and commitment of parishioners to share their time, talent, and treasure. As individual members of a family are essential to the communal life, your family is vital to the ecclesial life of the Church. Participating in ecclesial life is accepting your share of responsibility for the life of the family of God.

- Bernadette and Kyle have young children. To contribute to the life of the Church without having to leave the family at home, Bernadette volunteered to wash and iron the purificators used at Mass. Doing this service at home opens the opportunity for her children to help her do the special laundry for the parish. Their children's attention is heightened at Mass when they see the priest, and the Eucharistic ministers use the purificators that they helped launder.

The members of your family, prepared by the communal life at home, are ready to contribute to the ecclesial life. Family life helps members of your family to discover their gifts and gives them opportunities to use and grow in those gifts. Using the gifts that God has given you to serve the family of God is good stewardship of time and talents, and brings a sense of belonging to the parish community.

Spiritual Home

Integrating your family into the Church means enjoying a spiritual home for the education of your children. Because the Christian education you provide to your children is Catholic-based, the Church is your guide, and her teachings are your reference points for your family relationships and the education process. Your parish community is the Church on a local scale. Involving your children, particularly in parish life, impacts their faith formation and development. For most families, becoming integrated into your parish means going to Mass on Sunday. Though this is the essential part of Church participation and contribution, it is not the only way we are called to participate in the life of the Church. Participation in parish life largely depends on the stage of family life. Families with small children are in a different family stage in contrast to families with teens.

The parish community environment includes Mass, activities, actual parish structures, people, and your relationships. Your children will observe, learn, absorb, and orient themselves in this environment that includes the actions, language, attitudes, and culture of the parish faith community as they grow up. Everything in the Church has an evangelical, formational, relational, and a spiritual nature for its members, which is not lost on children. The figures, signs, gestures, music, church sacramentals, atmosphere, all speak to your children about the relationships with God the Father, Jesus, the Holy Spirit, and the People of God. In the spiritual growth and development that you and your children experience when engaging at Mass, the sacraments, and the community, your family gains a spiritual home.

Engagement in parish life is particularly relevant to the faith development of your children. There are many opportunities for families to contribute in the parish, such as serving as greeters at Mass or helping with a coffee and donuts social time after Mass. Most parishes offer faith formation classes for children and high school students. Many parishes need mature and committed Catholics to be catechists for these classes. For the teens in your family, it may be a challenge to keep them engaged in church activities and faith formation classes. At their stage of life, having peers involved in church activities is key.

There are many good Catholic programs and youth conferences to evangelize teens. Work with your priest and parish faith formation commission to bring not only good programs but also, Catholic disciples as youth ministers who have hearts to evangelize the youth.

- Josie and Tim are committed disciples, and they decided to put a priority on their children's religious education. Together, they decided that Josie would make the sacrifice of attending the ninety hours of training required to become a catechist for the Catechesis of the Good Shepherd (CGS), a Montessori approach to faith education. Josie volunteers as a CGS catechist at their parish, and their children attend different levels of this faith formation program.

On a broader scale, a spiritual home is a place where Catholics find the deeper meaning of life, a place where they can discover enduring goodness and beauty. Today, there is a real hunger for a genuine experience to love and be loved, and many who seek this can experience it in the Church where disciples are equipped.

- Often, converts to the Catholic Faith say they sense that they have "come home." There is a deep sense of completeness they now feel in being Catholic. The tangibles and intangibles of the Church speak to the body and the spirit.

The Church is the spiritual home of the family of God. Like most Christian homes, the door is open for others. In the Church, evangelization is going out to invite others into the life of Christ and his Church.

Evangelization

Integrating your family into the Church means active participation in her identity and mission. Jesus calls you and your family to actively engage in evangelization, to be instruments to advance the work of the Church, and to build the kingdom of God. The primary mission of the Church continues to be the proclamation of the Good News of Jesus Christ and to make disciples— so that all may know the salvation that Jesus offers. Because Jesus calls the heart of each person to be receptive to his love, each must choose to respond to or ignore this call. It is therefore crucial that everyone has the opportunity to hear the Good News; only then can he or she respond to the invitation offered. Catholics must carry their share of this work for the salvation of souls because it is the mission of Jesus. The new evangelization that the Church is engaged in today directs efforts to evangelize three groups of people:

1. *Catholics in the pew.* An invitation to a more intentional and personal relationship with Jesus.

   - Many parishes encourage parishioners to join small groups where they can continue their discipleship within a small community. Some people organize a small group themselves and meet in their homes.

2. *Catholics who have left the Church.* An invitation to renew their Catholic faith through discipleship.

   - The best approach is meeting one-on-one to identify any issues or the blocks that keep them from returning to the Church. Intercessory prayer is needed for them.

3. *Those who have no faith or those of other faith traditions.* An invitation to consider the claims of Jesus and the Christian faith

   - Respectful listening, along with a clear proclamation of the Gospel of Jesus, is needed.

Evangelization is about establishing relationships with persons because God loves each one, and you are sent to witness the love of God. The Holy Spirit is at work in the evangelizer as well as the one being evangelized.

For active missionary parents, evangelization may mean sharing the vision of missionary parenting for building the domestic church to other Catholic parents. Many couples and families need encouragement and support in raising their families today. Forming a community of Catholic parents committed to raising the next generation of Catholics can be a source of strength and hope for each other.

As Pope Benedict says, "To some extent, we are responsible not only for working out our salvation but the salvation of others. This all takes place between two poles: the great Church and the 'Church in miniature,' the family, in a reciprocal relationship."[18]

---

[18] Pope Benedict XVI, address on the feast of St. John Chrysostom, 2007

And Pope Francis teaches, "Families should not see themselves as a refuge from society, but instead go forth from their homes in a spirit of solidarity with others. In this way, they become a hub for integrating persons into society and a point of contact between the public and private spheres."[19]

The Making of Saints

Both the domestic church and the Church as a whole are in the business of making saints. Saints are the most beautiful creatures made by God because they allow the Holy Spirit to transform their hearts for love throughout their lives. They are open to the work of the Great Artist to conform them to his Son Jesus, docile to the action of the Potter to transform them in love, and submissive to the chisel of the Master Sculptor to form into reality what already exists in his mind. God, who is Beauty itself, creates beauty in his image and likeness in souls who cooperate with him. Mary, the mother of Jesus and our mother, is the Queen of All Saints. Her *fiat*—"Let it be done to me according to your word"—flowed from her being filled with God's presence—"full of grace." This fullness of grace with the presence of God makes Mary the most beautiful woman. Beauty is holiness, and holiness is love. Without holiness, one cannot be in heaven in union with God. Disciples of Jesus give their *fiat* to God, and this begins a work of transformation to beauty and love. Every saint starts with a relationship with Jesus, the opening necessary for the Holy Spirit to make a new creation. Saints also have a deep love for the Church and her teachings. Disciples aspire to become saints, and missionary parents desire their children to become saints. Saints meet the conditions for discipleship: "If anyone wishes to come after me, he must deny himself and take up his cross daily and follow me" (Luke 9:23).

No Perfect Saint, No Perfect Family

There is no mold to create a "perfect" saint. Each saint is an individual who lived in a particular time and place, and each came from a specific social and economic class, had a particular intellectual ability and personality. The common trait of every saint, though, is his or her faith in God, which includes hope in Jesus, love for others and the Church, and docility to the Holy Spirit. There are saints living today who live hidden lives of holiness and love. Although each of them is unique, their holiness is shaped by abandoning their

---

[19] *Amoris Laetitia,* 181

entire selves to Jesus and allowing the Holy Spirit to conform their hearts to Jesus and direct their actions. Saints know they are sinners. The more spiritually mature they become, the more aware of sin they are, and that drives them to the foot of the Cross to ask for mercy and forgiveness.

In the same way, there is no one mold for creating the perfect domestic church. Families are small first communities of faith that are unique and have a character all their own. The one common trait for domestic church families is faith—allowing God in their lives, nurturing a growing love for Jesus, others, the Church, and an openness to the leading of the Holy Spirit. Your holiness as a family will grow by allowing the Holy Spirit to form your hearts and direct your actions in love. As you and your spouse continue to mature spiritually and as your children grow in their faith, you will be more keenly aware of faults that miss the mark and hopefully, you more quickly bring yourselves to the foot of the cross of Jesus to ask for his mercy and forgiveness.

Repentance and transformation are ongoing processes in the interior life of the domestic church that nurture holiness. In the domestic church, the cross and resurrection are always near.

The Sign of the Cross

An external sign that often identifies Catholics is the Sign of the Cross. Prayers begin and end with, "In the name of the Father, and of the Son, and of the Holy Spirit. Amen." Sometimes, this is made as a gesture without words. Many sports fans understand the gestures of sports officials on the field that affect the game. The Sign of the Cross is not just a gesture, though—it is a sacramental, pointing us toward the sacraments. It can be efficacious, as when it is traced on the forehead of the one to be baptized to claim that person for Christ, or when the priest uses this sign when granting absolution in the sacrament of Reconciliation. The Sign of the Cross, then, is a gesture that is packed with meaning and power.

The obvious meaning of the Cross is Jesus' sacrifice for the forgiveness of sins, and Catholics proclaim this profound act in words and gesture. The vertical and horizontal movements reflect the communion with God and with the Church. The power of the Sign of the Cross, whether done by priests, religious, or lay people comes from calling on the name of God, "In the name of the Father, and of the Son, and of the Holy Spirit!" In acknowledging God's sovereignty and petitioning his loving presence, the praying person puts confidence in God's goodness. Calling on God's name is not only making a request to God, but it is also a submission to do his will. In making the sign over their bodies, Catholics surrender to the life of the Blessed Trinity in them.

When making the Sign of the Cross, be deliberate and intentional. As parents, teach your children how to make this gesture properly and reverently. In itself, it can raise one's heart to God. Likewise, teach your children how to genuflect before the Blessed Sacrament. They need to know that Jesus is present today for them. Gestures involve movements by the body that is not meaningless. Knowing why you make gestures and prayerfully doing them unites your body, mind, and soul that both express and deepen your faith.

Deny Yourself, Pick up Your Cross, and Follow Jesus

Today's families are busy, busy, busy, and there seems to be no slowing down. There is not just a seeming shortage of time for parents but a shortage of energy. The big temptation when attending Mass or participating in parish life is to do the minimum, leaving the rest for others to do. There is no substitute, though, for integrating your family into the Church and participating in parish life. The word *church* means "assembly." It is a convocation—a call to gather together. Who is calling? God the Father, Jesus who is present and encountered in the assembled, and the Holy Spirit, who gives divine life through the sacraments. God called the first assembly at the foot of Mt. Sinai, where he established the Israelites as His holy people. Imagine being an Israelite and not being in that gathering; it meant you were still in Egypt. Again, there is no substitute for Church.

Denying yourself means putting aside other non-essentials for your family so that your family can experience integration in the life of the Church. Say *no* to something of less importance to enable adding something of greater importance for your family. Establishing a hierarchy of priorities means rearranging of your family's time, efforts, and resources. Picking up your cross means listening to the leading of the Holy Spirit where your family's gifts are needed in the Church, whether at the parish level or out in the secular world. After discerning, commit to it.

To follow Jesus is to love his body, the Church, and teach your children to love the Church. The bottom line is that the Church needs your family, and your family needs the Church. Catholics must not take the Church for granted.

Many kings, rulers, and persons in the Old Testament longed to see the birth of the Church. The Messiah has come and is present in the Church today.

River of Life

Prophets in the Old Testament prophesied about the Messiah and the Holy Spirit, whose presence the Church enjoys today. Towards the end of the Church's liturgical calendar is the unusual Feast of St. John Lateran, a feast for a cathedral building rather than a saint or an event in salvation history. The feast day commemorates the first basilica in Rome consecrated in the year 324. The first reading at Mass on this feast is the vision of the prophet Ezekiel while the People of God were exiled in Babylon. He has a vision of a river that begins "flowing beneath the threshold of the temple ... and empties into the sea, the salt waters, which it makes fresh ... Along both banks of the river, fruit trees of every kind shall grow; their leaves shall not fade, nor their fruit fail. Every month they shall bear fresh fruit, for the flow from the sanctuary shall water them. Their fruit shall serve for food, and their leaves for medicine" (Ezekiel 47:8-9, 12).

This vision of the prophet Ezekiel was given to bring hope to Israel for their salvation and restoration in their exile, but its true fulfillment is seen only in the coming of the Messiah, Jesus. The Church now lives in the New Covenant, and this life-giving river flows today. It is the gift of the Holy Spirit poured out upon the Church. This is the River of Life from which all those who have faith in Jesus the Messiah drink and from which you and your family members drink. As the *Catechism* says, "Through the Holy Spirit we are restored to paradise" (CCC 736). In the Garden, God created every seed-bearing plant and every tree with seed-bearing fruit (Genesis 1:29).

Ezekiel's vision of the River of Life in whose banks are fruit trees of every kind is actualized today in the fruitfulness of family trees that are centered on Jesus and the Church in the Holy Spirit. When domestic churches are integrated into the Church, the presence of Jesus and the power of the Holy Spirit bring God's divine life into families. Grace made available in the sacraments and other means that the Church provides bears fruit in family relationships that will impact not only your family today but also the succeeding generations of your family. "Until the Spirit from heaven is poured out on us. Then the desert will become an orchard, and the orchard will seem like a forest" (Isaiah 32:15).

TIME TO TALK

1. Renew your commitment to the Catholic Church.

2. Do we give a good witness to our family and others regarding the Mass, the Church, and her teachings?

3. What can we do today for our family to get involved in parish life or community life?

PRAYER

Lord Jesus, thank you for your presence in the Holy Eucharist and in all the sacraments of the Church. Help us to love your Body, the Church and guide us to serve in the way you desire. We pray for the unity among Christians for which you prayed. Keep us close to you always, in your name we pray, Amen.

CONCLUSION

"What can you do to promote world peace?
Go home and love your family."

—St. Teresa of Calcutta

The Greatest Is Love

Recall the young boy named Augustine who was mentioned in the Introduction of this book. Try to envision a more grown-up Augustine as a thirteen-year-old seventh grader. Will he have a concept of an interior and spiritual life? Will he know Jesus personally, and will he have a prayer life? Will he identify himself as a Catholic? Will Augustine's chances for affirmative answers to these questions be greater if his parents embrace their irreplaceable roles as first educators and teachers of the faith? The likelihood for affirmative answers increases if parents do act to establish a domestic church, because children respond to genuine love found in strong family relationships. If Augustine's parents do not raise him with the home-court advantage in the domestic church, sadly, the chances are great that Augustine, even at a young age, will search for something outside of the family and Church to quell his restless heart.

Jesus Christ – Hope of the Next Generation of Catholics

By capitalizing on the God-designed beauty of the parent-child relationship, parents seize the natural advantage in raising their children in the Faith. It is the best and most effective approach to helping our children grow up with faith, hope, and love of God to equip them as the next generation of Catholics.

This book has presented you with a vision for missionary parenting in your domestic church, the first faith community for your children. The vision consists in establishing and maintaining six Christ-centered relationships. It is in relationships that a person, young or old, continues to be transformed, because love is expressed within relationships. Consider the beauty and power of these relationships in which Jesus is active:

- In discipleship, Jesus brings about the internal *unity of body and soul* within a person that original sin fragmented.

"Man fully alive is the glory of God." –St. Irenaeus

- Marriage as an *intimate communion of persons* becomes possible in marital spirituality where Jesus is at its center, restoring the ruptured relationship between man and woman.

  "There is no greater force against evil in the world than the love of a man and woman in marriage." –Cardinal Raymond Burke

- Missionary parents take on their irreplaceable roles of first educators and teachers of the faith to their children, so that their children can grow as *whole persons* being capable of responding to Jesus' call to be *united to him.*

  "Be who God meant you to be, and you will set the world on fire." –St. Catherine of Siena

- Jesus draws family members into a *communion of persons* ordered by family spirituality.

  "The future of the world and of the Church passes through the family." –St. John Paul II

- To integrate your family into the Catholic Church is to join the *communion of Christ's body* with him who is the Head.

  "That they may all be one, as you, Father, are in me and I in you, that they also may be in us." –John 17:21

The domestic church is the first and best means for evangelization of your family. The right ordering of relationships with God, others, and self brings about the fullness of human life and development. A good marriage, a peaceful family, and an interdependence with the Church based on the right order of relationships is a joy-filled life that is worth your effort of sacrificial giving. The hope for our families is a life with Jesus.

CULTIVATING THE SIX KEY RELATIONSHIPS ESSENTIAL TO YOUR DOMESTIC CHURCH

"Unless the Lord builds the house, they labor
in vain who build" –Psalm 127:1

I f you have the desire and a vision of what your family can be, you also possess authentic hope of developing a plan that will take you and your spouse towards that vision. The ideas in this book are only points of departure. You and your spouse can design an appropriate plan for your family that has the key relationships and essential components of a first faith community. Only you know where each of you and your family members are in spiritual maturity, along with the circumstances and significant challenges facing your family. It is time to honestly assess a baseline of where you are strong or weak in each of the six relationships. Sit together and discuss realistic goals for strengthening or establishing the key relationships for the next year. Using the schemas as aids to your planning, gradually incorporate essential components that may be missing—always aware that each schema begins with Jesus Christ.

Be the seed that dies and grows deep roots. Sow bountifully into the faith's fertile soil. For seed-bearing fruit, plant your family tree by the River of Life. Fruit-laden family trees provide food and shade for others, and each singular beauty gives glory to God who creates it.

CONCLUDING PRAYER

Lord God, we entrust ourselves and our family to you. Please
stir up the Holy Spirit in our hearts and in our family. We
ask for the intercession of Mary and Joseph for the graces to
become a holy family. We ask in Jesus' name. Amen.

ACKNOWLEDGEMENTS

We thank the many people who shared their gifts with us to make this book a reality. Thanks to Darcie Tallman, who willingly read through early developmental stages of the manuscript and provided critical feedback. Thanks to Frank and Elizabeth Rozycki, who read the book together and gave us invaluable feedback as a married couple. Thanks to Judith Leonard, for her unconditional support that encouraged us to complete this work. Many thanks to Mike Fontecchio of Faith and Family Publications who welcomed this project and helped guide us through its publication.

We are grateful to our parents, Robert and Ann Horton and Valentin and Marcelina Agatep, who brought us to the waters of Baptism and raised us in the Faith. We thank our children for their patience with us throughout the writing and production of this work. We thank the Holy Spirit for the vision and inspiration that grace the pages of this book.

ABOUT THE AUTHORS

Bob and Nannet Horton are members of St. Thomas Aquinas Church and Catholic Student Center in Ames, Iowa. Daily, they strive to live out their marriage vocation as faithful Catholic disciples. There are seven children and eleven grandchildren (so far) in their family. Bob is a Distinguished Professor of Soil Science at Iowa State University. Nannet is a homeschool teacher, a Family of the Americas Natural Family Planning teacher, and a Catechesis of the Good Shepherd catechist. They serve on the Marriage and Family Life Advisory Committee of the Archdiocese of Dubuque.